Always on Sunday

Tom Harpur
Always on Sunday

Toronto
OXFORD UNIVERSITY PRESS
1988

CANADIAN CATALOGUING IN PUBLICATION DATA

Harpur, Tom.
Always on Sunday

A collection of the author's columns originally pub-
lished in the Toronto Sunday Star.
Bibliography: p.
Includes index.
ISBN 0-19-540650-8

1. Christian life – 1960– . 2. Christianity – 20th
century. 3. Church and the world. I. Title.

BV4501.2.H37 1988   200   C88-093314-3

Cover design: Jeffrey Tabberner
Cover art: John Fraser

© Tom Harpur 1988
OXFORD is a trademark of Oxford University Press
1 2 3 4 – 1 0 9 8
Printed in Canada by Webcom Limited

For my father, William Wallace Harpur, who was born in Co. Tyrone, Northern Ireland, and who, after over thirty years in business, studied and was ordained as a priest of the Anglican Church of Canada. At the time of his death in 1968 he was the Rector of St. Thomas' Church, Millbrook, Ontario, and Rural Dean of Cavan.

"Faith of our fathers, living still . . . "

Acknowledgments

Writing in the daily press on values, morals, and religion, in the widest use of the term, is a delicate, sometimes perilous, task. I can think of few things in media more challenging—or, at the same time, more rewarding. My readers across the country have been of enormous help through a constant stream of letters, whether in commendation or in criticism. It is this feedback that is the lifeblood of any column. And so to them, my thanks.

As with my previous books, *Harpur's Heaven and Hell* and *For Christ's Sake*, my editors at Oxford University Press were a continuing source of encouragement. To Richard Teleky, the managing editor, and Sally Livingston, who worked most closely with the manuscript from start to finish, my sincerest gratitude.

Finally, I want to thank my wife, Susan, for her uncommon common sense and her unflagging willingness to listen. While I must take responsibility for the columns themselves, she has been my first and ablest critic.

Contents

Hast thou not known? hast thou not heard, that the everlasting God, the Lord, the Creator of the ends of the earth, fainteth not, neither is weary? there is no searching of his understanding.

He giveth power to the faint; and to them that have no might he increaseth strength.

Even the youths shall faint and be weary, and the young men shall utterly fall:

But they that wait upon the Lord shall renew their strength; they shall mount up with wings as eagles; they shall run, and not be weary; and they shall walk, and not faint. —ISAIAH 40:28–31.

Introduction

Synchronicity has become a very fashionable word these days, and rightly so. It refers to those unexpected, meaningful coincidences that seem to occur with inexplicable frequency at certain key periods of one's life. Coming most often when our consciousness is in a heightened or even an altered state, they seem to fit together too neatly to be pure chance.

Carl Jung, the renowned psychoanalyst, spoke of synchronicity as an acausal, connecting principle at work in the universe. Peter Russell, in his book *The Global Brain,* says that where this kind of felicitous "happenstance" occurs it often appears that the environment is acting in a supportive manner. Far from being random events, synchronicities seem the product of a benevolent force or intelligence. Our ancestors would have referred to all this as the work of Providence, or God.

In any case, I want to begin this book by acknowledging the impact on my life of what now seems to me an even more significant synchronicity than it did when it occurred, exactly twenty years ago. I have described in some detail in my first book how boredom and frustration with my job as a seminary professor, coupled with a conviction that the Church was failing miserably to communicate its message in modern terms, led me, in 1971, to become the religion editor of Canada's largest newspaper, *The Toronto Star.* It was the most important decision I had ever made and one that was to bring me a sense of fulfilment and adventure I had never dreamed of. For the first time it was possible not just to have ideas but to know the resources were at hand for carrying them out. But it is unlikely any of it would have happened as it did had it not been for an incident that took place in my study at the college in the spring of 1967. I was trying to mark some essays, but my mind kept drifting off to other things. I had become increasingly convinced of the need for Christians to stop all the insider-talk about spiritual realities and to grapple instead with the problem of addressing ordinary men and women, in terms they could understand, about issues that touched their daily lives most deeply. So I was sitting and pondering how I could become involved in some way in mass media. Suddenly I was roused by an energetic knocking at the door. I walked over, opened it, and found an Armenian gentleman standing there, beaming broadly and anxious to come in for a visit. His name was Albert Noradoukian. I knew him only slightly; we had been introduced one night after church by two students, his daughter and her fiancé, who came regularly to hear me preach. As I have since got to know him over the years, I would say he is one of the most original people I have ever met, with a style and joie de vivre uniquely his own. He makes superb handcrafted jewelry for a living, and excellent wines for moments of celebration and hospitality. And he is a keen Christian, though most unorthodox.

Albert sat down in one of my beat-up easy chairs, looked around at all the shelves of books for a moment, and then came straight to the point: "Tom, I've been thinking about this a lot and I've come to the conclusion that you should be on radio and television talking about religion and faith. These are mixed-up times; the clergy who are in the mass media around here don't seem to believe in anything much; so it's your duty to get in there and pitch!"

I was struck with surprise that he should just show up without announcement and at the precise moment when I was thinking about the very topic he wanted to discuss—and said so.

"Well," he said. "The real point is—what are you doing about it?"

I replied that I had been praying about an opportunity to get into media in some fashion for several months.

"That's exactly your problem," he retorted with some excitement. "You've got to stop praying about it at once!"

Knowing even from our first brief meeting that Albert was given to rather enigmatic aphorisms, I waited for him to continue.

"It's not a time for praying, it's a time for doing," he said.

A little impatiently, I pointed out to him how difficult it was for an outsider to know where to start. The Toronto media scene was, I knew, one of the most competitive and difficult markets to break into of any in North America.

Albert interrupted my litany of reasons why what he was proposing was difficult, if not impossible, with a theatrical wave of his hand: "Tom," he said (he likes using your name to silence dissent), "let me tell you a story. You know the New Testament account of Jesus' raising of Lazarus in the Gospel According to St. John?"

"Look, Albert, you and I both are aware that I'm the Professor of New Testament and Greek in this college. Of course I know the story of Lazarus. What is the point?"

Not one whit abashed, he continued as though I had said nothing: "You remember what happened when Jesus came to the cave-tomb where Lazarus was buried?"

I gave another impatient "of course."

"What happened next?" he said.

"Well, Jesus commanded Lazarus to come forth and he came out of the grave with the shroud still wound around him."

"Not so fast, my friend," said Albert, with a smile that was beginning to irritate me. "What did he do before that?"

I thought for a moment. "I suppose you're referring to the part where he tells the bystanders to remove the stone from the entrance to the tomb?"

Albert slapped his knee and, fixing me with his most piercing glance, cried: "That's it!"

By now I was about ready to tell him I had other, better things to do than listen to his riddles; and yet I was intrigued by his chutzpah. I motioned for him to get on with it.

"If you take the story literally, then we can assume that anyone who could raise the dead also had the power to remove the stone by himself. All he would have had to do was to issue an order and poof—off comes the slab. Just like that! Instead, Jesus tells them to remove the stone for themselves—and that's what God is saying to you: 'You've got to remove the stone yourself.'"

His meaning was beginning to dawn on me, but by now he was in full flight: "You say you want to get into media; well, how many newspaper editors have you made it a point of knowing? How many TV or radio producers have you ever taken to lunch? What kind of ideas or proposals have you got for entertaining, informative viewing, reading, or listening? You've got to do something, or you'll still be praying about it ten years from now!"

Obviously Albert was right. It was a time for the moving of stones.

The next day I contacted the only media person I knew (and him not very well), and in less than ten days I was on the air with the first edition of "Harpur's Heaven and Hell," a weekly, hour-long open-line show on Station CFGM in Richmond Hill, Ontario. Everything I have written or broadcast from that day on has been influenced by that experience. And I have had a love affair with all aspects of mass media ever since.

Reflecting on all this two decades later, I have realized that Albert's fortuitous challenge to me had a deeper, Jungian significance as well. He could have used any number of other approaches to spur me into action, but he chose the story of Lazarus. Looking back from my present vantage point, I now realize that in a very deep sense the decision to leave my official role in organized religion and espouse journalism was, for me, a real resurrection. I experienced a dramatic awakening in that my creative juices—the "Lazarus factor"—were lying buried and came to life. Without exaggerating, it was like being reborn.

When I eventually resigned as religion editor of the *Star*, in September 1983, I was granted a year's leave of absence to promote my book *Harpur's Heaven and Hell*, and to write *For Christ's Sake*. But even then I had the feeling I would not be going back. I had indeed interviewed almost everybody who was anybody in the field of religion over the preceding twelve years. I knew it was time to stop quoting others and say and write what I thought myself about spiritual and moral values, and about institutional religion. I wrote the book on Jesus and told the paper I wouldn't be coming back full-time because I intended to make my own way as an independent writer and broadcaster. Subsequently, when I was invited by the *Star* to do a freelance Sunday column, in the fall of 1984, I was eager to start. Soon it was syndicated in other newspapers from St. John to Vancouver and mail began flowing in from all over the country.

Believing as I do that true religion deals with the depth dimension of the whole of life, no subject was off limits, from the scare over pit-bull terriers to the controversies surrounding *in vitro* fertilization and surrogate motherhood. Readers have expressed pleasure and surprise over the broad range of subjects tackled. What follows here is a compilation of the best columns that have appeared over the past three and half years—always on Sunday.

I

SPIRITUAL ODYSSEY

Faith

Fundamentalists in all camps—Protestant, Catholic, Jewish, Islamic—share a number of admirable qualities. They are marked by energy, dedication, and singleness of purpose. They also share a number of flaws, however, and most of them stem from having succumbed to one of the human spirit's deadliest temptations. They have been seduced by the lust for absolute certainty in a realm where no such certainty is possible.

I am not concerned here to catalogue all the various problems, for themselves and for others, that flow from this crucial error. Still, it does explain the fear that seems to lie behind fundamentalists' unwillingness to question any one particular belief in their overall system: that if one part crumbles, the entire edifice will tumble down.

We must look at something deeper. Since at the moment it is this aspect of all religions that appears to have the highest public profile, most "outsiders" to religious belief and practice are being misled about the nature of faith in God. Faith is being portrayed as if it were some kind of sure bet or proven knowledge with an iron-clad blueprint for a happy, successful life both here and hereafter—the ultimate insurance policy, guaranteed by the oft-repeated slogan, "It's in the Book." The catch is that you have to read the Book their way; otherwise it's no deal.

But suppose you are one of those many people who can't accept this approach. Suppose you are unwilling or unable to believe two impossible or contradictory things before breakfast each day. You are convinced that, in the event there is a God, such a being would never require the amputation of your mind as a condition for worship or service. What do you do?

You can meet the fundamentalists' appeal with a phrase many have used in writing to me: "I guess I just wasn't born with the gift of faith." Or, as the majority have done, you can simply turn off religion altogether. This is a great tragedy—and entirely unnecessary.

Faith matters very much to me. I believe in one creator God who is "above" us all and yet in us all. I believe in "the resurrection of the body, and the life of the world to come." For me, though, faith does not mean swallowing absurdities or blinding oneself to anything that hints of evidence to the contrary. It does not mean freedom from, or fear of, doubts. Its content includes much more than intellect and reasoning; but it is never irrational. The word I would use for this aspect is "non-rational" or intuitive.

We "know" and commit ourselves to God not wholly because of logic, nor wholly because of some flash of insight or intuition, but because of a unique blending of both. It is an act of trust by the whole person. That is why Jesus and the Torah speak of loving God with all one's heart, soul, strength, and mind (Luke 10:27). Rather than leading to smug complacency or conveying a granite-like "proof" of anything, faith is supremely a matter of risk and adventure.

Because we hate ambiguity and the unknown, many of us would prefer it if there were some force—some infallible book or pope or guru—that could twist our intellectual arm behind our back to the point where we'd have no choice but to cry uncle and submit.

But that's not the kind of faith the Bible speaks of. Abraham, the great example of faith for Jews, Christians, and Muslims, had no absolute certainties when God called him to leave his home and begin his historic trek: "He went out, not knowing whither he was going." It was an act of trust and risk. Jesus Christ, in the Garden of Gethsemane, had no sure, unerring certainty of what God's will would finally be, no blueprint— just radical commitment. Otherwise all the agony, the cross, the desolate cry of God-forsakenness, was simply a charade. That some believers insist on claiming what Abraham and Jesus never had strikes me as bizarre. God continues to seek or pursue every one of us, like Francis Thompson's Hound of Heaven, as we flee "down the labyrinthine ways" of our own minds. We must not let the earnest but distorted sense of faith held out by extremists put us off the real thing.

Good and Bad Religions

Many zealous believers feel compelled to differentiate between "true religion"—theirs—and "false religion," by which they mean yours or mine. Yet the truly fundamental difference is between good religion and bad. This key distinction cuts across all denominational or sectarian bounds. Its reality can be seen in all major religions in most parts of the world.

Bad religion operates on the basis of fear—fear of God, fear of life, fear of the future. True, our ancestors spoke of the "fear" of the Lord. But this fear was not inner dread; it was the sense of awe, wonder, or reverence felt in the presence of the Wholly Other—what is properly called a sense of the numinous. Bad religion coerces people into "being good" by scaring them with threats of what will happen if they're bad. Virtue is promoted in terms of rewards and retribution, not for its own sake alone.

It is the very soul of ethics that one tries to do what is right and good "because it is there" to be done. It carries its reward with it in the sense that it's the way life, human and cosmic, works best—even if at the time it means sacrifice. Bad religion, on the other hand, relies on the kind of guilt that corrodes the heart of all it touches. A constant theme of readers' mail is the way so many, rather than finding healing in their religion, have been wounded by the burden of sin and guilt it has laid on them.

Legitimate guilt has a function. To err against oneself or others is naturally to invite some remorse. But good religion deals with this quickly; it offers the possibility of a change of heart and forgiveness more generous than the mind can span. It abhors any suggestion that guilt and other human weaknesses be used as subtle levers for manipulation or control.

Bad religion fears freedom. Unquestioning obedience is praised as the highest form of dedication. Doubts—which are normal, even essential, steps to spiritual growth—are labelled "assaults of the enemy" and vigorously repressed.

Bad religion sees enemies on every side. Depending on the context, these may be the media, the humanists, the communists, the intellectuals, the theological liberals, the allegedly "anti-life" forces, the feminists, you name it. Beware of any faith that defines itself in terms of what it is against.

Fundamentally, all bad religion is opposed to authentic

human maturity. It wants desperately to keep its adherents as dependent children ruled by the deputies of an authoritarian male deity—forever and ever, Amen. Yet the Bible's message is that the Creator Spirit we call God summons us to an ever fuller adulthood, to fuller freedom, fuller humanity. We are to be more than sons and daughters of the Lord of life. The call is to be co-creators in shaping a more truly human existence in harmony with our planet.

The Jewish Bible (the Old Testament) is about liberation, wholeness, and the healing of the nations. It's about loving God with one's total being. In the New Testament, Jesus' radical challenge is the same. The King James Version (Matt. 5:48) has him say: "Be ye therefore perfect even as your father . . . is perfect." But the Greek word of the original, *teleios*, does not mean morally perfect. It was a term much loved by Aristotle (who began as a biologist) and used by him to describe an organism that has come to its full potential—for example, a mature oak as contrasted to an acorn. Jesus is saying: "Become fully what you are meant to be. Be self-realized, as God is." St. Paul had the same vision. He never loses sight of the destiny of the human. Using the same word, *teleios*, he says plainly that the final aim of Christian living is to come to "mature humanity," as seen in and measured by Christ (Ephes. 4:13).

Belief

At a party recently I saw a friend who has been an atheist for the fifteen years I have known him. I have always had respect for his position. The reason is that he is a true atheist. In other words, his convictions have been reached after much reading and thought. He's not one of the run-of-the-mill, lazy-minded braggarts who wear their supposed atheism on their sleeve but never really think much about anything, let alone God or metaphysical truths.

As far as the poseurs are concerned, it is better not to cast pearls before them, as the Bible warns. But you can argue or converse meaningfully with a fervent rational atheist. You can even admire the courage or the will of those who face life, and ultimately death, with no sense of a living God as their present help and future destiny.

There are two things I want to make clear, however. First, atheism, which comes from two Greek words meaning "no god" or "without god," is itself a form of faith or belief. You simply cannot *prove* the non-existence of God. Like the theist— one who believes in God—the atheist has a creed whether he or she likes it or not. At its heart lies an "I believe," or an act of trust. To turn it around once more, the statement that there is no God cannot be empirically verified. It lies beyond the senses and thus beyond the reach of science altogether. The atheist lives *sola fide*, by faith alone, just as much as Martin Luther did. Second, respect him or not, I firmly believe the atheist is wrong. In our society, thankfully, he has the right to be wrong.

Before I say why I think the atheist is mistaken, though, I want to deal with another, much larger group: those who call themselves agnostics. Here again is a word that comes from two in Greek, and the literal meaning is "I don't know." Agnostics say they remain suspended—unable either to believe or not to believe. They greet all talk of religious truth with a raised eyebrow or a large question mark. They can't decide. Agnostics also can be divided into a minority who try to keep an open mind, and who have read and thought enough to know what the issues are, and the majority who are really perpetrating a hoax. These have no more idea of why they doubt than many Christians have of what it is, or why they do, believe. Their agnosticism is nominal, a mere pose.

One has to respect the true agnostic, but it has always seemed to me that agnosticism is, at bottom, polite atheism. You can suspend judgment, but in the meantime you have to act, to live, to make decisions. Not to have decided about the God question is to have decided as far as immediate, practical issues are concerned. Perhaps a better phrase than "polite atheism" would be "practical atheism."

The belief that atheism of whatever stripe is wrong and that there is a God "in whom we live and move and have our being" is not, as some suppose, the child of blind faith or wishful illusions. It flows from the brain as well as the heart, from logical thought and observation as well as from intuition and the gift of insight. In the most modern terms, such faith is a product of both left-brain and right-brain activity. It comes from two kinds of knowing—the one rational, the other not irrational but non-rational, immediate and direct.

There is, to be sure, a "leap of faith" involved; however, it is a leap made not in spite of but because of the evidence provided by intellect and emotion. To believe that the miracles now being revealed by the biologists and the astronomers are just the result of a cosmic crapshoot or blind chance takes more faith than I can muster. And what the intellect affirms the human heart usually confirms too.

This does not mean an end to questions or to the doubts that, squarely faced, often lead on to deeper faith. By no means. Nor is there any magic to which theists have access while atheists do not, no matter what the TV preachers say. What it does mean is finding that what St. Augustine once said is true: "Thou hast made us for Thyself and our hearts are restless until they find their rest in Thee."

"The Lord Is My Light"

There are times in the lives of people close to you, friends and relatives, those in your office, on your street—times, perhaps, in your own life as well—when the pain and suffering seem overwhelming. To discover true comfort and inspiration at such times, one does well to seek out the wisdom of someone who has suffered even more deeply, and won through. One such is the unknown author of the biblical Book of Psalms.

There is no aspect of the human condition the psalmist doesn't know or deal with. He knows first-hand about physical illness, emotional upsets, fear, depression, God-forsakenness. Yet through or at the end of it all, his faith and hope in a loving God at the core of the cosmos triumph over every evil. My favorite verse in the entire Bible comes from Psalm 27:1: "The Lord is my light and my salvation; whom then shall I fear? The Lord is the strength of my life; of whom shall I be afraid?"

Notice the confident affirmation that whatever life gives us to contradict it, however meaningless things seem to be, there is ''the Lord'': a creating, sustaining divine Mind or Supreme Intelligence in and through and beyond the millions of galaxies and the minute complexities that make up our universe. There is no proof possible for such a bold assertion. But, as millions since have also testified, the author says his deepest instincts, intuitions, and insights into the realities of life convince him it is so—"closer than breathing, nearer than hands or feet."

"The Lord is my light" . . . The Psalmist, like most of us, did not see visions, hear voices, or receive other supernatural signs. Nevertheless, he says that God is his light. The Latin version rightly translates this "light" not by the simple word *lux*, but by the word *illuminatio*. The Lord, he says, is the one who illumines the whole of reality for him. He is speaking not just of his sense of God's guidance in daily decisions; he means as well that knowing there is a "Lord" at the center of existence makes everything else radiate with meaning. The truth that the universe is not empty and indifferent to our agonies, that even suffering can be made to yield some ultimate good, however dimly perceived as yet, that death itself is not the end, brings comfort and encouragement—a release from darkness. It is the difference between night and day.

" . . . *and my salvation* . . . " The word "salvation" doesn't mean much to most of us today. But the reality intended by it is vital to us all. It means wholeness, mental and physical. It means health in the profoundest, widest possible sense. The ground of our being, the Lord, is concerned with the totality of our existence both here and hereafter.

If you read enough of the intimate devotional outpourings in the Book of Psalms, you realize that the author is aware that much of life, at times, seems to deny God's salvation. But you learn too that this is no unexamined faith, no Pollyanna dreaming. He has searched the depths as well as the heights and has tested his convictions in the crucible of living.

Finally, we see that, like Jesus later, he recognizes the final enemy as fear. Knowing the Lord is his light and his salvation brings him deliverance from this ancient foe: "whom then shall I fear?" And in saying "whom" he also includes "what"—in other words, there is nothing and nobody to fear in the end.

That is the ultimate message of all true religion. Or, as St. Paul movingly puts it: "I am fully persuaded that neither death nor life . . . nor anything else in the whole created order shall ever be able to separate us from the love of God . . . " (Rom. 8:39).

The Easter Message

As the name itself reminds us, Easter is about the miracle of the whole created universe; it is about the cosmic context in which we all "live and move and have our being." According to Bede, the ''father of English history'', (A.D. 673–735), the word "Easter" derives from Eostre, an Anglo-Saxon spring goddess. In fact the celebration of Easter has taken the place of a much older pagan festival, which welcomed the rebirth of nature. The giving of Easter eggs and the symbolism of the Easter bunny, though some Christians regard them as frivolous, commercialized hype, actually serve to remind us of this crucial link with the basic truths of fertility, birth, and seasonal cycles. At this level of meaning, Easter belongs to everyone.

There is another level yet at which this day speaks powerfully to persons of every creed and place, but before turning to that we must see its specifically Christian message. At the core of Christianity lies fervent testimony to a miracle. As Peter said, in his first recorded sermon: "This Jesus hath God raised up, whereof we are all witnesses."

Make no mistake. From a purely human point of view, Jesus' ministry ended in a catastrophe. He became the victim of the same hatred of "subversion" that haunts those who oppress and mutilate humanity today. He was tortured and impaled on a gibbet by the powers of the status quo. He was denied and abandoned by his closest followers. So much for the Kingdom of God! So much for the power of love! If that is where the story had ended, Jesus would probably never have made it into secular history at all. The Gospels would never have been written; Paul would never have composed his letters. This is why Easter was the pivotal, indeed sole festival of the Church in its earliest days and why it still is, theologically speaking, the *raison d'être* of Christianity.

The "good news" of Easter Day was, is, and always shall be that the same, fully human Jesus who was crucified, and tasted death, was then seen alive in a radically transformed, spiritual body by the Apostles and other believers. And while I, as a Christian, believe in the truth of the Resurrection, there is another facet to the Easter message and symbolism that touches us all, Christian or not. As in Tolstoy's great novel *Resurrection*, at issue here is the theme of personal renewal or resurrection. We all as human beings need to be born again. Not in the now-clichéd sense of the so-called Born Again movement. Not just once, as in some road-to-Damascus conversion. We need to be born again—and again, and again.

What has always amazed and inspired me, both in my years in the parish ministry and ever since in journalism, is the way quite ordinary people can rise, be born again, from disasters or trials of all kinds, and do extraordinary things. The deepest meaning of Easter is that the power to transcend our limitations, to be reborn in the face of any problem or tragedy, is available to those who seek it. Life can begin again, no matter what "crucifixion" or sorrow we have known. This may be the greatest miracle of all.

The Christmas Message

Christmas, like Easter, is a cosmic festival that rightly belongs to every person on the face of the earth. It resonates with the music of our total belonging to the solar system and our galactic home, the milky way. It touches the heart of everyone. Its message is not just for this or that group of committed Christians. It belongs to that vast majority called nominal Christians; to Jews and Muslims, Buddhists, Hindus, Sikhs, and all those of other faiths; to countless millions whose faith is in the state, material things, or nothing particular at all.

Its themes are universal, and not even the ringing of cash registers or the cacophony of canned Christmas songs can drown them out. In the silent night and in the breaking dawn they speak for all those who have the ears to hear the angelic singing.

In fact, in its beginnings Christmas was literally a cosmic celebration. There was no celebration of the birth of Christ for the first three centuries of the Christian era, and to this day scholars have never agreed on the precise date (either day or year) of the "first Christmas" in Bethlehem. The earliest Christians had little interest in Jesus' birthday; the principal focus of their concern and worship was Easter.

The first mention of celebrating December 25 in Jesus' honor comes from the Roman Church in A.D. 336. There is no doubt that the festival was inaugurated and thus dated to oppose directly the pagan feast of the *natalis solis invicti*, the birthday of the unconquered sun. To understand the instinctual wisdom—some would say, divine guidance—of this daring theft from paganism, one has to be aware of just what it was the pagan priests were celebrating.

The ancients were worried because the sun seemed to be losing strength as the days shortened to the December 21 solstice. "Solstice" means, literally, "the sun stands still." Thus fires were lit to lend the sun vigor; special rites and intercessions were made so that the sun might "rise again." Feasting and merry-making marked the realization that once again the days were growing longer. The sun had proved *invictus* once again.

For Christians, then, the day marked the birth of Jesus as "the Sun of Righteousness." But what this meant was that the Christian festival was squarely positioned within the planetary and solar rhythms. It thus gained a cosmic reference point—a power and energy and meaning far beyond itself. In celebrating Christmas we celebrate our cosmic connection, our deep nexus and bonding with all other species, all other aspects of our universe, our total environment. We celebrate the victory of life-giving light.

At the same time we celebrate the divine within us all. "In the beginning was the Word . . ."—so begins the haunting "Hymn to the Logos," which introduces John's Gospel and is always the passage read at Christmas. The idea that there is a cosmic "word"—sound, vibration, or, as the Stoics put it, a rational principle or divine fire, that comes forth from God and "lightens everyone who comes into the world"—is found in the Vedic scriptures of the Hindu and in almost every other religion. When John says that "the Word became flesh" he is speaking of what happened in the birth of Christ as the archetypal example of what occurs in all of us.

As I have written at length elsewhere, the traditional mythos or story of God becoming a human being in Jesus is, at its deepest level, a way of saying that God has become "enfleshed" in every person. It is this divine spark that, paradoxically, constitutes the essence of our true humanity. It is this same divine seed or light (religion speaks of it in a thousand ways) that makes us all "of one blood under the sun," whatever our race or creed or politics.

It is this "light" that gives each his or her ultimate value and creates the demand for justice on earth. It is because "we are all God's offspring" that "peace on earth, good will to all" is not a pious wish, but a divine imperative.

Soul Hunger

The army recruit was asked by his superiors to list his religious affiliation. He wrote confidently, "C. and E." The officer in charge tore the paper in shreds and roared at him: "You mean C. *of* E., Church of England, idiot!" The recruit shook his head and retorted: "No, it's C. and E.—Christmas and Easter, sir."

The young man was part of a large and increasing segment of the Christian population whose visit to church on Easter Sunday will be the last time they darken a church door until December 25 rolls around once more. A significant number of the world's approximately one billion Christians don't make even this nod towards their nominal religion. It's not that they feel hostile towards religion or spirituality. We are actually living in a very spiritual age; people are searching for depth and meaning in a world that sometimes seems to have lost its sanity.

The more affluent we in the West have become, the lower our spiritual standard of living has fallen. The Ethiopians and others in poorer nations suffer physical starvation. We languish from soul hunger. Life in our culture provides us with plenty of bread and circuses; it shortchanges us—or we allow it to—when it comes to nurture for our innermost selves.

The feeling I discern in many who have dropped out of regular church-going is that they had gone too often to this particular well only to find it had little or no water in it for them. What is being said and done in the services each Sunday either makes no sense or seems irrelevant to both the inner hunger and the stress and conflicts of everyday living. In the worst cases, the religious enterprise comes across more as a barrier to spiritual development than as a help.

The clergy, no doubt, are trying their best. I have nothing but respect for those who, day by day, faithfully care for the sick, visit the shut-ins, and administer the sacraments. But too often, when they mount the pulpit on Sunday, they have little that is truly meaningful to say.

Sometimes when I am sitting in the pew during a sermon and some particular inanity is solemnly pronounced, it is all I can do to keep from jumping up and shouting: "Why are you insulting our intelligence?" Few other public speakers in our society can get away with orating for twenty or thirty minutes without being challenged or questioned.

In his pulpit, however, the preacher remains aloof from and beyond rebuttal, and, short of risking being charged with interrupting a public worship service, there is very little anyone can do. Yet I guarantee that if the clergy knew there was a real possibility of being made to debate and defend their assertions, the quality of the sermons would improve immediately.

I remember once preaching a sermon on social justice at Little Trinity Church in downtown Toronto, a parish where I used to be honorary assistant while teaching at an Anglican seminary. At the end I said the usual prayer, collected my notes, and came down from on high. To my shock, the rector, Rev. Harry Robinson, now in charge of a parish in West Vancouver, had got out of his seat on the other side of the chancel and, striding into the middle of the church, was saying, "You can't leave 'er there, Tom!"

As the stunned congregation, mainly university students, suddenly awoke out of the torpor induced by my homily and began sitting on the edge of their seats, Robinson proceeded to dissect what I had said and to show why it was more or less ecclesiastical garbage. Not being one to remain silent and risk being thought a fool when there was such a good opportunity to prove it, I joined heatedly in what I thought was a masterly rebuttal. Then the whole congregation joined in. When the religious tempest finally played itself out, it was nearly an hour later. Nobody had left to check on the roast at home.

To Robinson's surprise, and mine, the opinion was unanimous that church had never been so interesting before. The strong implication was that we should repeat the performance every Sunday. We never did, but the thought that we might do so kept people coming—and staying awake during sermons—for many months. I don't suggest that other preachers follow this particular pattern; it's not good for the blood pressure. But no politician or other would-be persuader and molder of people's minds and opinions has such a passive audience at his feet every week. It's a fantastic opportunity to do something about the current spiritual malaise. Just getting up and pronouncing, in sermon form, what often amounts to the dreary "minutes of the last meeting" is not good enough.

I left the ordained ministry (though technically, in Anglican theology, "once a priest always a priest") not because of lack of faith, but because of a conflict of interest between allegiance to a bishop and my role as a journalist. I am often asked, however, what I would do differently if I were ever to return to active parish ministry. The answer is easy. I would spend more time listening to those outsiders I referred to at the start, especially young people. The clergy has more to learn from the disenchanted about how to communicate with modern people, and what their real needs are, than it will ever learn from hobnobbing solely with the already converted. In the Bible it's always the straying sheep that get the most attention.

At the same time, it is vitally important to bridge the enormous gap between what the experts know and believe and what is relayed to the ordinary pew-warmer. I would try to bring my parishioners up to date on the best contemporary biblical scholarship—mainly Roman Catholic, and much of it unorthodox—particularly regarding Jesus.

I would refuse to become involved with raising money, erecting buildings, organizing who can use the parish hall, saying prayers at the dedication or cornerstone-laying of public buildings. I would try to encourage my people to join with me in our common spiritual quest: to find within themselves the spiritual resources God has already put there rather than looking to me or the church to lay some trip upon them from above.

Above all, I would want my preaching and teaching to be an affirmation of the essential goodness and fullness of humanity that lies within each and every person, waiting to be realized. The churches have put far too much emphasis on sin and guilt. If people could hear more of the "yes" of God to their lives, there would not be so many millions saying "no" to religion.

Spiritual Healing

After finishing my hospital visits one afternoon when I was a minister, I was stopped on my way to the elevator by a couple who were deeply distraught. They explained that the woman's mother was in a deep coma and not expected to live. They apologized about not having any "church connection," but wondered whether I might have a moment to "say a few words" over her.

The request was too serious to refuse. I found the private

room where the patient, unconscious and surrounded by an oxygen tent, was gently ebbing towards her end.

It was one of those occasions, all-too-frequent for a priest or pastor, when I felt quite helpless, even out of place. Nevertheless, I reached in and took her by the hand as I said a brief prayer and recited that moving passage where Paul says that nothing, not even death, can ever separate us from the love of God (Rom. 8:38-9). The woman gave no sign of life other than the faint movement of the bedcover with her shallow breathing. I had a few words with the couple and then left, grateful to be on my way.

Since I had to be back in the hospital the following morning on another call, I dropped by the same room, expecting the worst. To my surprise, the woman was now fully conscious and knew who I was instantly, although we had never met before. She told me she had heard the words of the prayer and reading even though she had been unable to move or to regain normal awareness. And she said that immediately afterwards she had felt filled with an incredible sensation of light and peace. Whatever happened was so meaningful to her and yet so indescribable, she was only able to whisper: ''I never experienced anything quite like that before." She passed away later that same afternoon.

My reason for telling this story so many years afterwards is not that I believe in any kind of magic. Still less is it because I think I had any mystical healing powers. I haven't—though I believe there are those who may well do so. However, the experience had a profound effect upon me and my ministry while I remained in the official clergy. For one thing, I never again made any prior judgments about what sick people can or cannot know (particularly hear) while in a coma or other form of deep trauma. For another, I made the laying-on of hands, with prayer, an integral part of any contact with those who were ill. It never took the place of full medical care, and there were no miracles. But I came to know it as one of the most satisfying aspects of my pastoral role.

What is significant today is that the medical profession is rediscovering the healing benefit of an approach to illness that incorporates this very ancient, basic rite. *American Health Magazine*, in a recent feature, tells how health professionals are practising the laying-on of hands in hospitals and government-supported researchers are studying its benefits.

At New York University, Dolores Krieger, a professor of nursing, teaches "therapeutic touch"—a modern version of the centuries-old practice—to her classes. She centers her mind on a "compassionate intention to heal" and, moving her hands around the patient's body, hovers over areas where she senses accumulated energy. Conveying a feeling of well-being to the patient, she tries to promote health by redistributing the energy. The benefits seem to include reduction of pain, relief of anxiety, and improved blood chemistry.

The U.S. Department of Health has just awarded a University of South Carolina nursing researcher, Janet Quinn, a grant to study whether this therapeutic touch can aid heart surgery patients. Quinn reportedly is using as a working hypothesis the theory that "some kind of energy exchange" may be involved.

Some people will simply dismiss the apparent results of such experiments as examples of the "placebo effect." But that is one of those answers that raises as many questions as it solves.

Why does the power of suggestion work so effectively—if indeed that is what it is? And what about the woman in the coma who, as far as one can tell, was beyond suggestion in the usual sense? There is much more to all this than skeptics imagine.

Rituals and Spiritual Truth

The other morning was one of those exhilarating, high-pressure days we often get in a Canadian winter—no clouds in the sky, the snow snapping under your feet, the air clear and cold as water from a mountain spring. I was walking with my dog, Morgan, on a long tramp over hill and dale. There was nothing but snowdrifted fields, woods, and rolling hills in any direction.

Suddenly a large jackrabbit zigzagged up a slanting meadow towards some dense bush. Since a wide valley lay between, and the hare was within easy reach of cover, I was surprised at its obvious panic. It was running as if for its life.

Then I saw them coming: a pack of five brush wolves in hot pursuit. I had sometimes seen their tracks before, but in six years of hiking this same terrain I had never laid eyes on one. They were fanned out in an attempt to corner their quarry. But one actually stopped for a few seconds and, sitting among the stumps of an ancient hedge, watched Morgan and me with extraordinary, quiet intensity. Then he loped off and, like the others, quickly vanished after the intended prey.

Because all this happened quite quickly, and because the wolves were downwind from us, Morgan missed the whole episode. It was only when we had trudged and floundered through the drifts to where the pack had passed that he caught the scent and made a brave show of following the tracks—for a while.

Like you, I hope the jackrabbit eluded his pursuers. But that's not the point of telling this. As I reflected on it, the incident threw light on a matter of some spiritual depth: that is, the relationship between human beings and religious authority. For me, it helped to illumine the great difference between second-hand acceptance of religious truth and the self-authenticating, direct experience of it oneself. Here's what I mean. I have always known there are deer, wolves, and other "wild" animals in the wilder regions of the high ground between Lake Ontario and Lake Simcoe, where we live. Even an amateur naturalist like myself can tell that from the various signs—tracks in the mud or snow, animal droppings, and so on; in the case of deer, there are even road signs indicating crossing areas. But signs of deer or wolves are one thing; seeing the animals themselves is something else entirely.

One of the major errors people make with regard to religion is to take the "signs" of the reality at its core for the reality itself. Instead of seeing creeds, dogmas, rituals, hierarchies, or sacred scriptures as means to an end, as important but still secondary, they suppose that such elements constitute the sum of spiritual truth.

They see them not as signs that a reality whom we call God exists and can be known, but as the essence of God's being and will. They ignore the biblical injunction against all forms of idolatry—the putting of anything or anyone in the place of God.

It is this mistaken giving of ultimacy to secondary issues that is at the heart of all religious hatreds and prejudices today, as it has been through the ages. It has often justified horrific violence. The First Crusade, for example, in 1096, was marked by the slaughter of thousands of Jews in Germany. The cross of Christ had become a bloody sword.

Now, if somebody comes to me and says, "I think that's an interesting tale about wolves and deer in your area, but I don't believe it," I would have a hard time proving I spoke the truth. I would be able to tell them where I saw the game in question. I could perhaps find some tracks and point them out. But, the doubter might argue, the tracks could have been faked; perhaps they were left by dogs; and so on. What the skeptic really needs is to have the experience of seeing, in his or her own way and time, what I have seen for myself.

The same is true of religion. Sacred scriptures tell of others' experiences of God. The "tracks" of God are there; thus they are not a bad place to look while searching for the real thing. Creeds, rituals, religious leaders, all are pointers of a kind. But nothing can take the place of one's own, inner journey or of the encounter of the "alone with the Alone"—our direct, immediate experience of the Presence of God.

You don't have to become a mystic; nor is the call to form one's own "church" in a holy huddle of one. It's a matter of not being content with spiritual hand-me-downs, of piercing beneath the time-worn packaging to find the gift inside.

Ecstasy

What we need desperately as a race and as a culture is more ecstasy. That's right, ecstasy.

I can hear the screams of protest already. Isn't that what most of our major ills stem from? Everyone is looking for some kind of pleasure "fix" to escape the boredom, the pressure, or the pain of living in the "rat-race" of North American society.

So we have the idiocy of most prime-time television, the mindless pursuit of sexual thrills, the illusory high of consumerism, and the various addictions to mood-altering substances, from alcohol to smoked cobwebs or whatever. People are looking for ecstasy, though they usually seem prepared to settle for a lot less. As T.S. Eliot put it, "We smile, but the agony abides."

Well, I'm not talking about ecstasy in the popular sense of

feeling some overwhelming, pleasure-induced state of mental or even spiritual exaltation. Not at all. My concern is with our need for ecstasy in a much more radical sense. Literally the word, from two Greek roots, means the act or condition of standing outside of oneself—outside of a particular pattern or tradition of thinking, outside of a particular code, culture, or fashion. A moment, or a mode, of stepping beyond what one is told to think, expected to think, trained to think—perhaps forced to think—by everyone with a vested interest in keeping us from thinking for ourselves.

Nothing makes tyrants tremble, not to mention ecclesiastics, image-makers, market researchers, or giant corporations, like the encouragement of that kind of ecstasy. As the ancient Greek said, "Give me the right spot to place my lever, and I can move the world." Give a person the spot from which he can view the whole of his own life or society from a new perspective, and a new dynamism is released. True creativity is unlocked.

This, in fact, is the secret behind the entire story of human development— the spiritual dimension to our physical and mental evolution. The true heroes of our species have always been those who dared to challenge the way we both were and saw things. They stood outside not just themselves but their contemporaries, their rulers, their accepted wisdoms. And they moved the world a nudge, a yard, a league ahead.

We live in a time when this kind of spirit, courage, or intellectual risk-taking is more essential than ever before. The threats are terrifying; the opportunities are almost beyond imagining. There is no field of the human endeavor free from the responsibility to practise ecstasy—traditional religions, corporate business, governments, universities, trade unions, or the various professions.

Take religion, for example. The world's major religious leaders today are like people standing at the bottom of a miledeep well. They look up and see a glorious but distant light. But they seem unaware how constricted their vision is or how unconvincing they sound when they imply that theirs is all the light there is to see.

Cultural philosopher Rev. Thomas Berry, who heads the Riverdale Center for Religious Research in New York, was correct when he told a seminar: "We cannot do without the traditional religions, but they cannot (as they now are) do what needs to be done. We need a new type of religious orientation." It will emerge only if religious leaders and those who follow them will defy the entropy of the past and move to where they can see not just fresh light but today's men and women as they really are.

The whole "story" of the universe and our place as humans in it has been transformed by modern physics, astronomy, and the other sciences. Any religion that ignores this transformation and goes on using thought models appropriate to primitive times is doomed to irrelevancy and extinction.

But the same is also true of business. The "microphase" style of thinking that dreams only of immediate maximum profits or of expanding assets and takes no thought for the "macrophase" —the impact of all of this on our wasted earth—is likewise doomed to eventual ruin.

As the Club of Rome and other prophetic voices have warned, when you make absolute growth the core fact of your whole economic system, a sudden confrontation with the brute fact of the planet's limits can be catastrophic. Either we will stand outside our old values and demands on our environment and pay the costs of less extravagant, less insane lifestyles, or the various natural systems will collapse and we will be left outside.

More and more, our consumer culture calls us to the dance of pseudo-ecstasy . The time has come to step outside for some radical ecstasy as well.

The Still Small Voice

One of the things I'm sure must frustrate the Almighty is the way many people, instead of taking responsibility for their lives, prefer to see themselves as victims. They suppose it is easier to blame or envy others than to make the tough decisions required to shape their own destinies.

This infantile temptation assails all of us at some point in our lives. But giving into it simply stores up misery for ourselves and those around us. The problem becomes quite glaring in the case of religion. Millions, it seems, prefer to leave their spiritual lives in the hands of others. They long to be guided in what to do, think, even feel.

They cling tenaciously to whatever their particular guru,

preacher, or other functionary tells them is the revealed will of God for them—it's so much easier than to have an original question or thought of their own. As a result they remain spiritually stunted and unaware of their own potential.

Not long ago I suggested we could all do with more ecstasy in our lives. I used the word in its root meaning of standing outside of oneself and noted that only by standing outside one's habitual thought patterns, background, cultural setting, routine way of looking at everything, is it possible to get new, creative insights into relationships, work—even the very meaning of one's own life. It is a cardinal route to spiritual discovery and to becoming more authentically alive.

But there is another, correlative way to authenticity of being that has been glossed over by institutional religions and yet remains essential to wholeness or—to use the religious term—salvation. For what of a better word, I call it enstasy, from the Greek meaning "to stand within." Jesus, you remember, said, "The Kingdom of God is within you."

After years of studying faith and how the soul finds God, I am convinced that it is chiefly by standing within oneself—by listening to the "still small voice" of God's Spirit in the center of our deepest selves—that we find and know the real will of God for us.

It is in this way that we stop conforming to the wishes and wants of others and become what we are meant to be. Artists, poets, novelists, musicians, and other creative people might express the notion differently, but they will recognize immediately what I'm speaking about.

Many people tell me they don't know what to do with their lives, or that they don't know where to begin to find God. The answer is the same in every case: you have to begin by standing and looking within. This is what Jesus meant when he said that when you pray you should enter "into your closet" and there converse with God. He was talking about the inner self.

You have to ask yourself, with radical honesty: What is my heart (soul, mind, or however you want to say it) really trying to prompt me to be or do?

Yet many people are afraid to do it. Perhaps they're afraid of the changes they'd have to make if they really listened. Perhaps they're afraid that the God their parents, church, or society taught them to believe in would not want them to do what would bring them the greatest joy.

Sometimes, because of some buried or repressed guilt for which they've never let themselves be forgiven, they don't truly believe that God accepts and loves them enough to want them to realize their most-cherished hopes or dreams. They go around in fear, always waiting for the other boot to drop, worrying that God is going to strike them down.

What a waste of talent, energy, and time!

There is a "lost saying" of Jesus that occurs in the Gospel According to Thomas, found with other Gnostic writings in the sands of Egypt, at Nag Hammadi, in 1945. It says: "If you bring forth what is within you, what you bring forth will save you. If you do not bring forth what is within you, what you do not bring forth will destroy you."

We do not know for certain whether this is an actual word of Christ. I believe that it is. In any case, it is very powerful and fits in exactly both with his saying about the Kingdom being within and with the idea of enstasy.

We are not gods. But we are the bearers of the divine light. We are the stable in which God is born. Look not elsewhere. You will find God within.

Can the Churches Find Resurrection?

The urgent question facing organized religion in North America at Easter is not "Did God raise up Jesus from the dead?" but "Can the churches themselves find resurrection?" Will they allow God to raise them from the current "death" of irrelevancy, vagueness, and general lack of impact on the inner lives of the vast majority of people?

Unless there is such a rebirth, renewal, or bursting forth from the tomb, they will end up one day as mere cultural relics of a bygone era, maintained by some form of heritage grants. People will attend services occasionally, as we now go to see various kinds of ethnic performances—Scottish sword-dancing, for instance. But this is a far cry from a living faith.

It is no use pointing, as some do, to the apparent success of the born-again movement and its high-profile expression by the television evangelists. This strident Bible-thumping is not the first wave of a Christian renaissance. Just as moribund patients often exhibit deceptive appearances of new vigor before the end, so too do religious movements headed for ultimate extinction.

Certainly the fundamentalists have many attractive qualities. In most cases their motives and sincerity are not in doubt. And, for those who find its rigid tenets acceptable, this system can be made to work—for a time. The real problem is that a starkly literalist approach to faith, God, and the Bible will ultimately let its followers down with a thundering crash. It is only a matter of time, given the current explosion of information and knowledge, until this approach will be untenable for all except the few whose dedication to naivety outweighs all else.

What, then, should the churches do? What direction should they take in order to "rise again"? The need for certain changes is virtually self-evident. First, the so-called mainline churches have done, and are doing, a quite remarkable job on some aspects of social justice—native rights, refugees, South African racism, and world hunger, to name a few. Where they are failing badly is in making contact with the deep spiritual hunger of today's men, women, and young people.

There is evidence from all sides that people are ready for some new kind of breakthrough where the human spirit is concerned. We know that the global crises facing us over pollution, famine, population, and the threat of war can only be resolved if our moral awareness begins to catch up to our leaps in technology. What we are looking for is leadership and inspiration of a kind the churches could give if only they understood and believed their good news more deeply themselves and could find words and ways to make it known.

The God of the Judeo-Christian tradition is more than God enough for us in a space age if only He can be liberated from the prisons of our man-made dogmas, creeds, and rituals. These need not be abandoned. What is necessary is simply to see them as they are—very partial and inadequate symbols and images of a reality we can never fully comprehend, but that pulls us ever forward.

Second, it is very soon going to be too late for action in the realm of ecumenism: the churches must begin now to let go their scandalous petty differences and live and act together as one body. They don't have to merge or meld into an undifferentiated mass. They do have to stop the nonsense about not recognizing each other's ministers, sacraments, and rites. They have to stop barring others from full communion at the altar. They must cease their political and economic aggression against religious and other rivals. All the churches' talk about ecumenism has become boring and irrelevant to outsiders because there has been far too much rhetoric and too little real progress.

Third, going to church, temple, or synagogue has got to be made a vastly more satisfying experience than it is at present, or the majority will go on staying away in droves. Sermons have to make more sense, be more in tune with people's genuine needs (instead of making folk feel guilty and then saying, "We just happen to have the remedy for that guilt"), and more open to proper dialogue or feedback. Hymns should be singable instead of two octaves too high for anyone but a boy soprano. Lessons from remote parts of the Bible should be dropped entirely or else fully explained.

Above all, there should be some free time for meditation or just sitting still. Most often there seems to be a conspiracy between minister, choir, and organ to fill in every available second with noise. No wonder it frequently seems so difficult to hear the quiet promptings of the Holy Spirit within.

The Need For Worship

When I was a boy I was taken to church for worship twice each Sunday. In fact, for a while I was a chorister. I can still smell the warm, clean scent of the freshly starched high collars and white surplices we were decked out in by the choir mother.

As a student for the ministry, and then for many years as a parish priest, it was my duty not just to attend worship services all the time but to lead them. Then, as a religion editor for over a decade, I covered the worship services of all religions at home and abroad. Now, as a freelance writer and lecturer, I no longer am obliged to attend church regularly or take part in formal worship.

Thus the question arises: "Why bother?" Or, at a deeper level: "Why would God want or need our worship?" We are naturally suspicious of anyone who needs to be told how great they are. Indeed, if you think about it long enough, the concept that the Creator needs to be constantly admired, praised, and flattered is quite bizarre and contradictory.

But suppose—despite all the apparent efforts by religions over the years to "play up to" God in the hopes of cajoling favors—that the need for worship is not God's: suppose it is our own.

As one considers the vastness of the galaxy-strewn heavens, the wonders of nature here on our earth home, or the richness of all that we mean by humans-in-relationship-with-others, one becomes aware of an aching to express a sense of wonder and of gratitude. At times we are taken unawares; some unexpected glimpse of beauty, some act of love, some sound of music, or of children playing, takes us briefly into another realm. We are aware of being for a moment "at the still point of the turning world," as T.S. Eliot says; at a point of the intersection of time by the timeless. Or, as a friend of mine is fond of saying: "We hear the angels sing."

Often, through sheer busyness or dullness, we may miss the way even the most ordinary things can be shot through with glory. Francis Thompson put it this way:

> The angels keep their ancient places;
> Turn but a stone and start a wing!
> 'Tis ye, 'tis your estranged faces,
> That miss the many-splendored thing.

The human spirit longs at times to express in some, however inadequate, way its sense of the ultimate mystery that lies behind, and in, and through the "many-splendored thing." It is the deep-down response of every person who has ever tried to pray. How terrible it would be, say on a lovely morning in May, thigh-deep in a rushing trout-stream, fishing, feeling thankful, and having nobody, no One to thank!

I believe there is a "numinous" or divine dimension to the whole of reality that evokes in us the need to answer back with praise and joy. The theologians call it the *mysterium tremendum et fascinosum*. God awakes in us a sense both of awe and of allurement. When Moses saw the burning bush, others may have seen only a desert shrub with the sun behind it. He alone saw the vision and heard the words: "Take off your shoes, for the ground you tread upon is holy."

One of the best examples of this experience outside of scripture is found in Kenneth Grahame's children's classic *The Wind in the Willows*. Two characters, Rat and Mole, are wandering in the woods. Drawn to a clearing by a haunting piping, they suddenly feel they are in the presence of God. They become rooted to the ground by a sense of awe and longing. They feel astonishingly at peace, yet in that presence their muscles turn to water and their heads are bowed.

Rat asks Mole if he's afraid. Rat, "his eyes shining with unutterable love," replies: "Afraid? Of Him? O, never, never! And yet . . . O Mole, I am afraid!" Then the two animals crouching to the earth, "did worship."

Clearly, you don't have to go to church to worship. But it can provide a fitting context. The sad thing is that so many people forget—or never realize—that they can do it anywhere.

Inner Growth and Self-Examination

Socrates said that the unexamined life is not worth living. In other words, the secret of inner or spiritual growth, maturity, and happiness lies in asking oneself questions—honestly and regularly. What kinds of questions? Questions about our real motives, our true goals, about the kind of people we are, and about the ways in which we need to work at changing our thoughts and behavior. Questions, too, about the meaning of our work, our relationships, our ultimate destiny.

Because they have never learned to focus their lives in this way—or through sheer apathy and laziness—many people merely drift through life. They are sometimes plagued by a nagging sense of remaining unfulfilled. Often they are overcome by bitterness or boredom with themselves and others. They don't grow up because they have never exerted themselves to try. They fulfill the ersatz beatitude: Blessed are they who expect nothing, in the area of spiritual growth, for they shall never be disappointed.

Nobody can lay out a blueprint of the kind of self-examination most helpful to any and every individual, because we all have different needs and strengths. And we all start from different places. Still, there are some tried and true basic questions we all must wrestle with, and they make a first-class spot from which to start.

Over the centuries, millions have been helped and deeply challenged by three questions posed by Rabbi Hillel, who led an important school of Judaism at the time of Jesus. Hillel asked: "If I am not for myself, who will be for me? And, if I am only for myself, what am I? And, if not now, when?"

The first question deals with the profound truth that each of us has a primary responsibility for our own life. One of the greatest and most constant temptations of our age is to shift this responsibility to others. The secret of mental and emotional health lies in realizing that we alone are ultimately responsible for how we feel and for who we are. Blaming others is the beginning of neurosis.

Incidentally, one of the weaknesses of traditional Christianity is that it has somehow made people feel guilty about genuine self-love. Yet nothing could possibly be clearer than Jesus' statement that we are to love our neighbor exactly *as we love ourselves.*

Hillel's second question challenges false self-love, the infantile, selfish narcissism that looks only at "what's in it for me." To be truly human means to care for and be involved in the lives of others.

His third query, "If not now, when?", strikes at what psychiatrist Scott Peck (*The Road Less Travelled*) calls spiritual entropy—the torpor of wishful thinking that procrastinates, delays, and avoids tough decisions. How much human happiness goes down the tube because we promise ourselves we will change, love, do what our best thought has always been prompting, relax, enjoy our children, partners, friends—but always in the future.

If there is one thing all the sages, philosophers, and spiritual geniuses of all time agree upon it is this: either live each moment to the full, doing promptly what your highest self keeps whispering, or be prepared for frustration and, in the end, the most tragic thing of all—regret. "If only I had done . . . " is a very sad lament indeed.

There is a probing question posed by Jesus, which has come echoing down the ages and is peculiarly relevant in our success/celebrity-oriented culture: "What shall it profit one to gain the whole world and lose one's own soul in the process?" It is easy to suppose this refers only to winners of lotteries, movie stars, the makers and shakers of business or politics—anyone, as long as it is always "the other guy."

But the question bears on the life of anyone who puts the achieving of personal or materialistic goals—the ideal family, the ideal home, the perfect sex life, the best score at golf or whatever—ahead of his or her own spiritual development.

A wise professor in my distant past once gave his students two questions, which I have personally found useful and now recommend to students myself. He said that in every area of thought or action it helps greatly to clear the mind if one asks, "What does it mean to be fully human in this situation?" And, "What is ultimate here? What is it for the sake of which I do everything else?"

Life After Death

I

I don't think there has ever been a time when I didn't hold firmly to belief in a new kind of life and being beyond the grave. My grounds for so doing have been—for me—both cogent and diverse. In the first place, this conviction has always been one of those deep inner intuitions about which one feels that if it is false, then everything else one thinks or knows is false as well.

Interestingly, the Greek root of the word "idiot" means "one's own"—in a sense, then, if such an intuition were merely a private idiosyncrasy, it could be termed a form of idiocy. However, the instinctual awareness that death is a gateway or birth into a new dimension of reality is probably the most widespread and ancient of all human ideas. It fulfills the traditional definition of a catholic or universal doctrine: *quod ubique, quod semper, quod ab omnibus creditum est* (what has been believed everywhere, always, and by all).

Then too, as one trying to be a Christian, I have as well a distinctively religious ground for my belief. If one takes the vision of God focused in Jesus Christ as one's supreme moral and spiritual authority, there can be no doubt about life after death.

Jesus' teaching and the evidence for his resurrection remain crucial testimonies here. As the great preacher Leslie Weatherhead writes in his brilliant book *The Christian Agnostic*: "What a note of authority there is in his words to one whom we miscall 'the dying thief!' Jesus is not dealing with a great saint. And a dying man talking to a dying man does not hedge or bluff. If Jesus had said, 'Well maybe we shall meet again, I hope so, indeed I have faith that it may be so,' that would have been as far as many would go today. But no! He, who knew more about the unseen than any of us, could not have used more definite language . . . 'Today, thou shalt be with me in Paradise.'"

This is not to say that I have never had any intellectual difficulties in this area. I remember vividly how, as a student, I had to wrestle with the concept of the resurrection of the body. Over the years, though, I have come to understand the meaning of those words. What they affirm is the truth that, whatever life after death may be like, we are not going to be disembodied shadows or spiritual essences of some kind. Just as there is a physical body—with all its limitations and imperfections—so there is an etheric, astral, or spiritual body.

Paul says the two are related, as the rotting seed potato in the furrow is related to the new plant. But they are not molecularly or in any other way identical. "This corruption must put on incorruption," the apostle says, for flesh and blood cannot enter the realm of the psychic or spiritual. Belief in this spiritual body eliminates all the scruples and worries of those who, because of a crudely literalistic belief in the resurrection of the body, feel that cremation is wrong.

The Christian belief in the resurrection of the body is not a belief in the resuscitation of corpses. It is rather the assurance that at death the whole person, body-soul-mind, will be transformed, or "put on immortality." I believe we will thus recognize one another in the world to come. What's more, we will be able to communicate and understand at a depth now granted only, if at all, in fleeting glimpses. Or in dreams and yearnings.

Unfortunately, the traditional language about heaven or the life to come is so off-putting that many people throw out everything in a reaction of disgust. I don't blame them—an endless church service is nothing to look forward to. Praying to be delivered from such an end, Weatherhead adds: "And if I and some of my friends are going to sing in the heavenly choir, it will not be heaven for anyone!"

Clearly all the imagery about harps and choirs and streets of gold is simply an attempt to describe the unutterable. What is really meant is this: If you think of the greatest beauty you have ever seen or heard—well, heaven will be like that, only more so. The promise is here: "Behold, I make all things new."

II

The preceding column on belief in life after death met with strong and articulate protest from some readers. One, taking issue with my statement about the deep intuitive sense most of us have that death is not the last word, suggested that I had mistaken wishful thinking for intuition.

How does one who believes that death is a door and a rebirth into a new dimension of reality or being respond to such criticism?

Obviously it is no answer simply to say that one believes in a life hereafter because the Bible teaches it or because Christian dogma says Jesus was raised from the dead. This has weight for me, as a believer. But none of it amounts to incontrovertible proof. In fact, we must go further and admit straight off that this is an area of human existence where there can be no such thing as proof in the normal, scientific sense of the word.

Nor does all the new material about Near Death Experience (NDE) or the current spate of testimonies about alleged past lives, à la Shirley MacLaine, constitute proof. The NDE only tells us about fascinating experiences some patients have had when close to death during cardiac arrest or other similar traumatic happenings. None of those reporting such experiences has really died. Their witness is interesting, but it may or may not be news "from the other side."

Similarly, hypnotic regression into alleged past lives *may* be evidence of immortality or reincarnation. But it also may be nothing more than a sign of the extreme fertility of human imagination or our ability, under changed states of consciousness, to tap into what C.G. Jung called the "collective unconscious" of the human race.

The same reasoning applies to visions of the dead, messages via spiritual mediums, and other apparently supernatural phenomena. Individually, none of these things—however powerful and convincing they are to those who experience them—amounts to absolute proof.

Nevertheless, we must say that together, and in conjunction with the near-universal belief in a life after death in all cultures, since the very dawn of human intelligence, these phenomena mount up to a persuasive cumulative case in favor of it. In other words, while it is a matter of faith, it is not "blind" faith. It is faith based upon a host of reasonable grounds.

What the author of the skeptical letter seems oblivious of is the fact that his unbelief is just as much—perhaps even more —a matter of faith than is the position he attacks. There is no scientific evidence that the human mind/soul does not or cannot exist after death. Indeed, all the foremost scientists I know of today are talking about mind as a spiritual reality existing alongside matter but independent of it. If anything is dead, it is the old materialistic, mechanistic view of reality.

Speaking of the mind and the will as non-material, a leading neuroscientist, Sir John Eccles, argues that they are probably "not subject in death to the disintegration that affects . . . both the body and the brain." That's what religion has been saying for centuries.

II

FAITH IN CRISIS

TV Evangelists

Each fall, at the University of Toronto, I teach a course on mass media and how they are to be understood from a religious point of view. Obviously this means spending some of the time scrutinizing the behavior of that proliferating new breed, the TV evangelists. In their attempts to study and evaluate the electronic preachers and their "cathode church," there are two major errors I warn the students against.

The first is failing to appreciate fully their positive side. These people understand the basic rules of communication in a way the mainline churches, to which my students belong, seldom have in the past and certainly show few signs of doing in the immediate future. The rules are these: have something to say; say it with the conviction that comes from being convinced oneself; go where the people you want to reach are (mentally as well as physically), and speak or act out a language everybody understands.

The TV preachers and their clan are determined to take modern media seriously. They are willing to take risks and to think big. Some twenty new religious radio stations are being opened every month in the U.S.; religious TV stations have increased from sixty-five in 1982 to two hundred and twenty-one in 1987. And at the 1987 convention of religious broadcasters the speakers included both President Reagan and Vice President Bush.

The second mistake I alert students to is more fraught with hazards for society in general and for the Christian religion in particular. It consists in not looking beyond the most obvious and most superficial shortcomings of the superstar preachers to the realities beneath.

It is easy to pour scorn on their endless obsession with dollars, or on the bizarre giveaway gimmickry—everything from pots of holy oil to statues of Jesus that glow in the dark—aimed solely at getting ever more names on the computerized mailing list. But surface criticism of an evil is often worse than no critique at all. It merely masks or, worse, legitimizes what is really going on. Too much purported analysis of the evangelists has been in this category, shallow and tepid.

The truly serious distortion at the core of the phenomenon of the electronic church is that it is a total caricature of what it so loudly shouts that it is all about: the life and teaching of Jesus. To discover the truth of this charge, all you have to do is to watch these "prime-time preachers" steadily for a few hours and ask yourself what their underlying message is—what are the key values they bless and promulgate? In most cases the list is bound to include:

- a rampant militarism based on an apocalyptic vision of the future—a vision which, by the way, is based upon a hunt-and-pick method of reading the Bible and a theology of fear and despair;
- success, often defined in the most crudely materialistic terms;
- the cult of celebrity, with all the worldly glitz and glamor it entails;
- a devotion to instant answers, a push-button Christ for a push-button age;
- a profound commitment to the U.S. form of capitalistic free enterprise as the only "Christian" economic option;
- a blind patriotism that blatantly equates God's will with the great American way of life;
- and finally, to go with this, utter dedication to the doctrine of social evolution. In other words, they would ban the teaching of evolution in the classroom, but accept a survival-of-the-fittest ethic for the marketplace: if you are poor it is really your own fault; those at the bottom of the heap don't try enough, believe enough, or give enough to ''the Lord's work."

Lowest of all is the preachers' use of guilt to make viewers feel they will personally be responsible for "unsaved" loved ones or others going to a literal flaming hell if the program goes off the air for lack of funds. That's the stick. The carrot, equally crude and equally unbiblical, is the promise of material success or "blessing" in return for cash.

These people wield the New Testament like a club while ignoring its most fundamental teaching: that to follow Jesus means to risk losing everything. In a current TV commercial Pat Boone, all smug and toothy, bleats that the book he is offering will lead to a worldly success like his. Jesus talked about struggle, lowliness, and a cross. In fact, while Jesus' teachings challenge the deepest values and structures of this and every culture, the message of the TV preachers does the very opposite. It seeks to sanctify every idol from militarism to the cult of celebrity.

In short, these preachers are not just innocently trying to package and sell religion as you would soap, or beer, or cars. They're peddling a set of social and cultural values that actually contradict most of what Jesus ever said or did. They have, to be blunt, succeeded in turning the essential message of Jesus inside out, or upside down. Don't just take my word for it. Reread the Sermon on the Mount (Matt. 5-7) yourself.

In Woody Allen's film *Hannah and Her Sisters* a character named Frederick watches a few TV evangelists at work and describes them as "third-rate con men." He continues: "If Jesus ever came back and saw what is going on here in his name, he'd never stop throwing up." Frederick has it right.

A Religious Summit

The world is suffering from an appalling lack of spiritual and moral leadership; yet millions more confess allegiance to God or Allah than ever before in human history. The time has come for the upper echelons of every creed and rite to acknowledge this tremendous irony and to dare to do something about it.

The first step, I believe, is one I suggested in a book in 1983, and was raised more recently by Most Rev. Robert Runcie, Archbishop of Canterbury: that the spiritual heads of all the chief religions meet at a major summit conference; the most appropriate site would be somewhere in the globe's worst trouble spot, the Middle East. I am not so naive as to think that the complexities of global tensions will be instantly solved just because religious leaders get together. But the idea holds a massive potential for moral pressure towards justice and peace.

The Pope and the Archbishop of Canterbury, both of whom are apparently fond of travel and spend much of their time patting their own faithful on the back, should take the initiative in setting up such a summit. Billy Graham should be there along with other major Protestant figures, such as the head of the World Council of Churches. Top rabbis from Israel, Europe, and North America should attend; so too should the leaders of Eastern Orthodoxy, particularly those from the Soviet Union. Islamic spiritual leaders must be there together with Hindus, Sikhs, and Buddhists. All of these say they believe in brotherhood, peace, and human rights. Yet all, willingly or not, consciously or not, are guilty of complicity in some form or other of violence and oppression.

The first few days of such a summit should be devoted to the participants' confession, collective and individual, of failure to insist on compliance with their high spiritual ideals and rhetoric, both on their own part and on that of their hundreds of millions of followers.

The world needs to hear the Russian Orthodox bishops condemning the Soviet terror in Afghanistan and the treatment of Jews and dissidents in the Soviet Union. Graham and other Christians from the West ought to be heard loudly and clearly tearing the mask from Ronald Reagan's bloody guerrilla war against the elected government and the people of Nicaragua.

It is imperative that Jewish spiritual guides, both within Israel and outside, be heard speaking out not just about Israel's right to exist, but about the issue of full justice for the Palestinians. The current cycle of horrific acts of terrorism followed by horrific acts of retaliation is spiritually, morally, and politically bankrupt. Muslim and Jewish religionists ought to be heard saying so.

The Pope and his clergy must be prodded to be much more forthright and consistent in their at-present tentative approach to IRA butchery in Ulster and Maronite violence in Lebanon. The Rev. Ian Paisley should be branded as promoting the opposite of what true religion is all about: reconciliation and tolerance. Sikhs and Hindus at the summit need to hear from the other leaders how the world sees the strife in India, as a total contradiction of everything Sikhism and Hinduism stand for.

Having fully admitted "before God and each other" the part their own faiths have played and are playing in world conflicts, the religious leaders could openly resolve to "walk in newness of life" and urge their followers to do the same. It would be a significant beginning. They would then be in an honest position to bring the kind of pressure to bear on political leaders that all their talk implies.

Harrowing Hell

No single concept in the long history of ideas has done more harm than that of a literal hell. Nothing has inspired more guilt and fear in the minds of young and old alike; few teachings have wrought more cruelty in the name of religion. Yet there are preachers in the tens of thousands and good, faithful Christians by the millions today who still subscribe to this grotesque and long-outdated notion. And millions of devout Muslims do the same. (Hell and its synonyms refer to a *spiritual* state of despair and of feeling cut off from God, from one's best self, and from others. Jesus seems to use this notion to underline the seriousness of the choices one has to make. It lends ultimacy to his challenge.)

But, unable—or unwilling—to tell the vast difference between the language of imagery, of symbol, paradox, and parable, and that of literal fact, these people persist in the bizarre idea that scriptual references to a "place" of eternal punishment actually describe a specific, existing reality. They believe, and in the case of the preachers, would persuade others, that a loving, merciful God will nevertheless permit the vast majority of humanity to endure a literal "lake of fire" prepared from the dawn of creation. They insist that God does this very reluctantly, of course; but He-She does it all the same.

Hell is the penalty for using our God-given gift of free will to make the wrong choices, so the argument goes. In other words, nobody is sent to hell. We allegedly opt for hell ourselves. It's the logical consequence of the sin of unbelief.

It may be traditional orthodoxy, but it is not true—and it is dangerous. Before detailing why, though, it is worthwhile illustrating more precisely what it is we're dealing with.

The Hebrew Bible (the Christian Old Testament) says next to nothing about a place of punishment after death. The idea did develop, however, in Jewish circles in the two centuries prior to the birth of Jesus. Thus a late hand added the words ending the otherwise glorious Book of Isaiah, words later echoed as a kind of formula by the authors of the New Testament: "And they shall go forth and look upon the carcases of the men that have transgressed against me: for their worm shall not die, neither shall their fire be quenched. . . ."

There are references to Gehenna or hell in the Gospels and lurid descriptions in the most imaginative book in the New Testament, Revelation. Here we are told that the devil is to be cast into the lake of fire and brimstone where the beast and the false prophet are and shall then be "tormented day and night for ever and ever." At the very end, death and hell itself will be cast into the lake of fire, together with "all whose names are not found written in the Book of Life" (Rev. 20:10, 14–15).

The Koran, written about five hundred years later, also has several vivid descriptions of hell. For example, Mohammed is told by Allah: "Verily, we have prepared for the wrongdoers a fire whose flaming canopy shall enclose them. And if they cry for help, they will be helped with water like molten lead which will burn their face. How dreadful is this drink and how evil the fire is as a resting place!" (Sura 18:30).

Throughout the ages, such flights of religious imagination and hyperbole, taken literally, have had an incredibly negative effect on people's understanding of God and on their treatment of their fellow humans.

Too often the traditional Christian or Muslim God with his ''hell'' is a monster God who tends to produce ''monstrous believers''—followers ready to do monstrous things to all heretics and outsiders. It's not accidental that U.S. President Ronald Reagan's current nuclear insanities are so hotly backed by the religious right. After all, what's a little nuclear hell here compared with what God has in mind for later? As Robert Short writes in his book *Something To Believe In*, the notorious cruelties of the Crusades and the terrible tortures inflicted by the Inquisition make sense and "even seem humane" in the light of hell: "If the number of souls who were to burn in the everlasting torment could be reduced by now burning to death a few hundred thousand heretics . . . then what could be more rational?" As he notes with sarcasm, this is murder, "but murder with a heart."

The doctrine of a literal hell should have been dropped centuries ago when the idea of the three-tiered universe on which it was based—heaven as the higher realm, earth as the middle plane, and the regions of hell below—was being shot to pieces by Galileo, Copernicus, and their successors. That it still thrives is testimony to the power of human credulity and fear.

Belief and Violence

A lot of people lately have been asking me why it is that religion and violence so often seem inextricably linked. Reading the flood of mail that greeted a recent column about Christian homosexuals, and realizing the full extent of the hostility and vindictiveness being expressed by these otherwise sweet Christians, has forced me to ask the same question.

Why is it that so many religious followers—in a variety of world faiths and sects—have been in the past, or are today, prepared to countenance virtually anything from torture to capital punishment and, ultimately, the use of nuclear weapons? The answer is that the kind of god or gods you believe in and worship determine the kind of person you will be. Inevitably, you come to resemble whatever receives your ultimate homage and devotion.

Put in its bluntest form, those religious believers who find it so easy and reasonable to condone violence are committed to a god whose nature is essentially violent. In fact, there are Christians of all denominations who in reality see God as a violent sadist—though they have never brought this fact to consciousness and would deny it instantly if it ever surfaced in their minds.

They talk about a God of mercy and of love without limits, yet see no conflict when they go on to argue that the wages of sin, as many letter-writers put it, is "death both in this world and the next." They write blithely, as we have seen, about the torments of hell and "the lake of fire" reserved, however reluctantly, by God for the "wicked."

Just how this eternal punishment is supposed to fit in with Jesus' clear teaching about God as a tender, forgiving parent they neglect to explain. Somehow they must expect us to believe that we are more moral than God—what sane human parent would punish his or her child "without end"?

Here again, the real reason behind the basically schizophrenic attempt to hold dogmatic allegiance to a god who is simultaneously perceived to be both loving and cruel is an overly literal, simplistic approach to sacred scriptures. For example, far too many millions of Christian believers have never yet been helped to see that there are many stages of moral and spiritual development in the Bible. The various authors, over the centuries, reflect greatly varying levels of insight into the true nature of the Creator. As even Martin Luther realized, all parts of the Bible may have been inspired, but some parts are much more inspired than others.

Luther called the epistle of James "a right strawy epistle" because of its strong emphasis on personal effort or "works," and he wasn't all that impressed with St. Matthew's Gospel either, because of its stress on keeping the law of Moses. There are places in the Bible where God is portrayed as commanding his people to commit acts that, in the light of other passages or indeed of our own consciences, we now think of as utterly immoral. The most obvious example is that of the order to commit genocide against the Amalekites and to wipe out even their cattle and pets.

The book of Psalms is rich in spiritual comfort and insight. But it is uneven. When the authors ask God to curse their enemies or speak of dashing the heads of their foes' children against the stones, we know we're back on crude tribal-deity ground once more. It is not only foolish but dangerous to suppose otherwise. What we have, then, is an emerging, ever-deepening understanding of God in the Bible. The climax of this comes for Christians in the vision of this ultimate ground of all being as self-giving love, the "Our Father" of Jesus' great prayer. It is just as contradictory to say that this kind of God sends AIDS as a punishment on homosexuals as it would be to allege that He is punishing the people who perish in the various earthquakes, plane crashes, and other catastrophes that the media report with such appalling regularity. But some of the earliest Bible authors would have had no problem with either statement. Taken literally, the story of the flood in Genesis would describe the deliberate massacre of both the guilty and the innocent on a scale that would make the earthquake disaster in Mexico City seem minuscule by comparison. And all by the hand of God!

I'm a believer, and one who is ready to learn from anyone who really knows. But don't ask me to believe in a god who is more spiteful, cruel and violent than Uganda's Idi Amin ever was. Surely we can never worship a deity who is less compassionate or loving than ourselves.

Nature's Fury

Most of us found it well-nigh impossible to get our minds around the slaughter of thousands of people by a killer typhoon and tidal wave in the Bay of Bengal on May 24, 1985. The final count of the dead may never be known; 250,000 were left homeless and cholera outbreaks soon added to the tragedy.

It is no help to say the people shouldn't live in such a flat, storm-infested region; that they should have known the risks since there have been thirty-two lethal storms there in the past twenty-five years; that they were aware 500,000 had died in the typhoon in 1970, or that they were warned this time, twenty-four hours before the disaster struck, that a typhoon was on its way. The president of Bangladesh, Hassain Mohammed Ershad, has told reporters the state could not order the evacuation of the most vulnerable islands in the bay because of population pressures on the mainland.

When the storm struck, the ill-fated nation had a population of 100 million in an area about twice the size of New Brunswick. With a growth rate of 2.7 percent, the total would increase in one year by 2.7 million—the population of Metropolitan Toronto. At that rate, it would have taken only five or six days to replace the number lost in the catastrophe.

"The island people heard the warning, but they had no place to go and no way to get there," said Iqbal Mujtaba, a Bangladesh navy commander. "All they could do was sit there thinking Almighty God would help them." The president made the same point: "Where could they go? They depend on God and just try their luck."

According to the *Los Angeles Times*, some of the more devout survivors viewed the cataclysm as God's (Allah's) punishment.

The country is overwhelmingly Muslim; the disaster struck during the most holy month of Ramadan. Thus, they concluded, God must be punishing them because of those in their villages who "have fallen away from Allah." How are we to come to terms with all of this?

One way, of course, is simply to blot the whole episode out by a kind of self-induced psychic numbness. To some extent we all do this in the face of the overwhelming litany of grief and misery communicated to us daily by the media; we need some emotional protection if we are not to be crushed by it ourselves and so left unable to be of help to anyone else. Yet such head-in-the-sand tactics only buy us time. They don't resolve the searing intellectual and religious problems raised by such tragedies. Those who believe in God and those who don't can agree at one level: the disaster, like the Ethiopian famine, or the killer tornado that struck Edmonton in the summer of 1987, can be explained in wholly natural terms.

A wall of water fifteen to twenty feet high, driven by fierce winds, will inevitably have a devastating effect on any highly populated, low-lying terrain, especially if the people live in flimsy huts. In spite of the recent tornadoes, we in Canada are fortunate in being largely free of such vast natural tragedies. Life, as they say, is not very fair.

But for the believer, no matter how casual, there is the age-old conundrum of what is called theodicy, or how to justify God's ways to humankind. Jews, Muslims, and Christians hold God to be all-knowing, all-powerful, and all-loving. Yet God permits the unbearable suffering of a woman watching in horror as her children are swept away in a mad rush of waters, of old people left homeless, with nothing to eat or drink.

The oldest "answer" to this dilemma is the one given by some of the victims just cited. It's as ancient as the story of Job and his would-be comforters: God is punishing people for their sins.

I reject this near-blasphemy with the same sense of outrage as Job did. The untold thousands—including babies—killed in Bangladesh or the thirty or so killed in the Edmonton storm were no more "sinful" than any of us. Besides, the image of a deity who keep records of our errings and lashes out in rage-inspired reprisals is crude, immoral, and a denial of all we mean by love. If we can see this, it makes us superior to such a god and deprives us of any reason why we should give respect or worship at all.

Elsewhere I have written about the problem of evil at some length. Here I will say only this: the cosmos was created according to "laws" of nature. This is why it is a cosmos, an orderly rather than a chaotic universe. The word "cosmos" comes from the Greek *kosmeo*, to bring order out of chaos. The same forces and laws at work in the Bay of Bengal disaster are those that make all scientific predictions, technology, and human existence on this planet possible.

If God were to keep interfering by some supernatural act every time water drowns, volcanoes erupt, winds blow, or bullets are fired, everything would fall into utter confusion and arbitrary chaos. It is the same force of gravity that keeps us all from flying off the earth into space that brings death if we fall from a highrise or walk off a cliff. Thus we can call a typhoon, a tidal wave, or a tornado an "act of God" only if we do so in this limited sense. Ultimately, such disasters bring us face to face with mystery.

Our response? In faith, we can commit those who have been killed to God's love and care. We can join with all others of good will to assist the survivors, financially and in many other ways. And we can pray that in the face of desperate calamity they may eventually know the miracle of saving hope again.

Religious Excess

The best-known, and still the least acted-upon, maxim of the ancient Greeks is "know thyself." Less well-known but just as crucial to civilized human existence is their saying "nothing in excess"—the literal translation of the Greek is "nothing too much." What is being praised and advocated here is a basic virtue that has been echoed by every major religion and philosophy: moderation or self-control.

Unfortunately, we live in a world where extremism often seems the highest value. As a columnist I have learned that many people are made very angry by the suggestion that they should practice tolerance. The worst cases are often those who make the most vocal claims to piety.

Religious extremism, stemming from the perverted view that the group or individual in question has the only, infallible truth about the ultimate mysteries of life, inevitably finds itself saying and doing things that wholly deny the core teachings of the original founder or prophet. Most often, the completely irreligious or agnostic person can see this with a clarity that eludes the religious fanatic completely.

It is quite simple, really. No moderation, no tolerance, means no love. Nothing exceeds like excess.

You can see it glaringly—and embarrassingly, if you are a Christian—in the extraordinary claims of the extremely right-wing, racist Afrikaner Resistance Movement in South Africa. It is not enough that the violence and repression directed against the black majority persist and increase as world denunciation mounts. The ARM and its supporters flaunt the symbols of Christianity as if they alone were the true defenders of the faith.

Their swastika-like cross, made up of three sevens (the supposed perfect number of the Bible), reminds one of the Ku Klux Klan. They see themselves as God's chosen people: in fact, they reinterpret the whole tale of "salvation events" in the Bible to cast themselves as the focus. Blacks are allegedly willed by God to remain "hewers of wood and drawers of water."

But Christians, alas, have no monopoly on extremism. Alarming stories out of Israel reveal an entire society threatened by chaos because of religious-secular strife. Not long ago, extremely conservative Jews set fire to or damaged over a hundred bus shelters in Tel Aviv, Jerusalem, and other cities to protest "indecent" advertisements showing women in skimpy lingerie or swimwear. The pent-up fury of secular Jews, who had long resented the amount of power wielded politically and otherwise by the ultra-Orthodox, then exploded in an attempt to burn down a synagogue, destruction of sacred scrolls and other religious objects, and the smearing of swastikas on the walls of the Great Synagogue in Tel Aviv.

Acts such as these by Jews against Jews make for sad reading. Premier Shimon Peres called upon Jews everywhere to "mobilize to extinguish the blaze" and warned explicitly that the nation, having withstood so much from without, could risk destroying itself from within.

Regrettably, at this moment Islam affords its own share of violence-prone extremism as well. In his best-selling book *The*

Spirit of Allah Iranian journalist Amir Taheri has given the world not only a detailed biography of the Ayatollah Khomeini but an intimate picture of life inside a theocracy—a state purportedly run according to God's will.

Taheri says that one of the reforms introduced by Khomeini is an amputation machine for cutting off the fingers and arms of convicted thieves. In an interview with *The Washington Post* the author said this bit of "technological progress" caused a big debate in Iran. Some mullahs were opposed to it because it makes the punishment less painful and therefore detracts from its effect. It is thus banned in some cities and used in others. First offenders are merely beaten. Repeaters get worse beatings and then begin to lose an arm: first a finger, then . . . Frankly, when this is "progress" you know something is dreadfully awry.

The good news is that each of the "true believers" cited here would do anything rather than admit to a single doubt they could be wrong.

I suppose there is something noble about being willing to die for a creed. It's the being willing to kill or maim for it that bothers me.

A New Inquisition?

Today, strange as it may seem, the Roman Catholic Church is making its own martyrs: the theologians. Not all of them, of course. Just those who dissent from or question traditional Roman teachings. The Vatican's powerful Congregation for the Doctrine of the Faith is hounding and investigating these teachers and scholars with an energy and persistence seldom seen since it went by another name—the Holy Office of the Inquisition. They are being stripped of their titles as Roman Catholic theologians, put under orders of silence, and harassed by procedures that would not be accepted in a secular judicial system. The situation raises acutely the question of intellectual freedom in the Church and threatens to undermine the credibility of its leaders when speaking out about the cause of human rights beyond its walls.

The saddest and most worrying thing about this centralizing

attempt to muzzle dissenters is that these alleged mavericks are the very thinkers most looked to by non-Roman Christians intent on renewal. And they are the lone sign of hope for millions of Catholics concerned about a relevant faith for themselves and their children. In fact, read out the names of those currently being cross-examined or disciplined by the Vatican's guardians of orthodoxy—Leonardo Boff of Brazil, Hans Küng of Tübingen, Edward Schillebeeckx of the Netherlands, or Charles Curran of the U.S., to cite a few—and you realize you are talking about some of the most creative minds in Christianity today.

There is a supreme irony here. The people who are being singled out and attacked for failing to come to heel whenever the Pope or his Number Two man, Cardinal Joseph Ratzinger, demand it are those whose lifelong commitment has been to the Church's central task: the communication of God's good news to modern women and men.

I must say I find a number of things to marvel at in this Vatican-versus-the-theologians matchup. First, John Paul II and Ratzinger seem to have succumbed to the notion that if you simply keep repeating tired or unacceptable formulae in ever sterner tones, the vast majority of the flock will knuckle under and admit that what they once found irrelevant, crude, or nonsensical is now clearly of God. Second, there is a totally false assumption behind most of the conservative arguments against the dissenters: that Rome's teaching on matters of faith and morals has remained eternally the same down through the centuries. But anyone with even the remotest knowledge of Church history knows this is not the case. Notable examples of change include the attitude to slavery, the teaching about papal infallibility, or, in our own era, the triumph at Vatican II of the principle of religious freedom itself.

Finally, the authorities in Rome, perhaps because of the setting and props from the past, seem to have no grasp of the extent of the crisis facing the Church. (Protestant and Anglican leaders suffer a similar myopia). The Christian Church may be growing in Africa, but in Europe and North America the decline goes on apace. The most striking development, though, is the way the Roman Catholic Church has suddenly caught up with a trend that for Protestants began just after World War II. During the past two decades, weekly church attendance for Canadian

Catholics (the U.S. figures are similar) has fallen dramatically from 85 to 45 percent.

Papal teaching on birth control is rejected by the bulk of the Catholic population here and throughout the industrialized world. Opposition is growing to the teachings on divorce and abortion. (It is significant that in the most fiercely devout Catholic country of them all, Poland, the rate of abortions and live births is roughly equal.)

Obviously no religious movement can simply tailor its beliefs to opinion polls—giving Johnny what Johnny will swallow. But there is such a thing as the *sensus fidelium*—the deep intuition of the laity as to what is right and true. A lot of Rome's current moral teaching goes against this awareness and so is doomed to rejection.

In sum, the progressive theologians are not necessarily always right. But they're not disloyal renegades either. Instead of attempting to suppress them, Vatican authorities ought to thank God daily for their insights and courage. It's time for a creative dialogue—not a return of the Grand Inquisitor.

Suffering

The winner of a recent—obscene—$10.2 million lottery prize in Ontario reportedly went out and bought a gold cross before anything else. Family sources said he wanted to express his thanks to the one who made it all possible. One can forgive his elation at the windfall fortune, but the kind of thinking, alarmingly widespread, that attributes lottery winnings or other events of that ilk to divine intervention is really a lot of heretical nonsense. It reduces God to a kind of arbitrary deity sitting on some heavenly throne doling out favors to a lucky few. Nothing could be less spiritual in concept, less just, less deserving of anybody's worship.

The corollary is also true. The Lord causes nobody's misfortune. God is not in the rewards-and-punishments business, dividing out bad luck, pain, grief, or any other kind of suffering to this group and not that.

Thus the question so often heard by doctors, therapists, clergy, or close friends of those in trouble, "Why me?", literally has no answer. There is no "why" in the sense that some divinity, power, or fate has deliberately sent us a specific misery.

I'm not saying we shouldn't try to use our reason to deal with tragedy and pain. It is essential that we do, and that we take all rational means possible to minimize it. But the way this life and our cosmos have been created, they include the factor of chance or random luck. Things can occur for good or ill to anyone. You could win a lottery; you could slip on a banana peel.

In any case, grief, suffering, and pain are universal, inescapable. We can try to deny this; we can follow the TV evangelists or the self-help gurus and attempt to trivialize it; we can blame others, or curse the heavens. But nothing changes. Suffering is part of being human.

Long ago, Buddha taught that life is suffering. Jesus said this world is such that trouble is inevitable; he himself "learned obedience through suffering." About five hundred years earlier, the Greek dramatist Aeschylus wrote that humanity's destiny is to learn through suffering.

What is truly remarkable, though, is the enormous capacity of individuals to meet and transcend such suffering. That is, they are able to accept it, not as a blow from a sadistic god, but simply as part of reality. It is there and they deal with it, moving somehow beyond it in a new way or forcing it, like Jacob wrestling with the angel, to yield up a blessing.

They didn't deserve it; they didn't seek it; they (to be honest) hated and dreaded it. But still they have been able to transform it by growing. The tragedies that could easily devastate or embitter are often transfigured as they are made into steps up the rock-face of maturity or doors into larger areas of service for others.

For example, as a former minister I know there is no greater loss than the death of a child. The shock is numbing; the future seems void; there is guilt, anger, and loneliness. I met just the other day with several bereaved parents who know this particular hell. Yet they are not paralyzed or in retreat from life. They are doing an incredible service. They are part of Bereaved Families of Ontario, which now has parallel associations in most of Canada.

The group began with the hopelessness of four bereaved mothers who met years ago at Toronto's Hospital for Sick Children. Realizing that only those who have been there can really understand this grief, they gradually formed a healing, compassionate network that has wrought near-miracles. People learn to smile again who feared they never would. Their loss is not forgotten, but somehow, through struggle and sharing, it is transcended into something that can only be called beautiful.

Nothing, I believe, is closer to the heart of true religion than the meeting of suffering in this way. Even if it never once mentions the name, it is done in the power and by the grace of God.

Institutional Coercion

A number of clergy and churches are now using a kind of emotional blackmail on people who don't attend yet still want some service or rite. For example, the non-church-going couple who request a traditional wedding are often made to feel they are religious lepers. They have to attend classes, services, the works, to get what they are really after. If they can jump through the required hoops, they still end up paying more for the actual wedding than those who are a visible part of the flock.

A little of this may be understandable. As the book says, "Marriage is not to be taken in hand unadvisedly, lightly, or wantonly." And somebody has to pay for the building to be there the rest of the time; somebody has to sweep up the confetti.

Still, there is far too much institutional coercion going on. People regarded as "outsiders" are being forced to conform. They do so only because their life situation or need makes them vulnerable to manipulation. For any priest or minister knowingly, or even unconsciously, to exploit this vulnerability is wrong.

The blackmail is yet more obvious and un-Christian when it comes to having babies baptized or christened. Thousands of parents are being compelled to take lengthy instruction sessions and to promise to attend and support the church in question. Otherwise the request for the child's baptism is turned down flat. I know from readers and my many contacts that frequently the denial is blunt almost to the point of rudeness. Formal religion, powerless in virtually every other way to make society do its bidding, knows it can still make this particular whip crack.

Certainly the church is entitled to set some conditions. Parents ought to find out ahead of time what it is they profess to be doing when they make baptismal vows on behalf of their offspring. And I can comprehend the irritation of clergy who at times feel they are being used by people to get little Johnny "done" so that they can bring the heirloom christening robe out of the mothballs, have a big family party, and finally satisfy the grandparents.

I well remember having to bite my tongue occasionally when I had a parish myself. In the middle of a hectic schedule you would get a call from somebody you had never seen or heard of literally demanding to have the baby done. Once or twice they had already set a date! There was a strong impulse to say facetiously, "Yes, and how would you like the little nipper done—well, medium, or rare?"

But in those days we never refused anybody. The service itself quotes Jesus' saying: "Let the young children come unto me." In fact, I baptized so many babies some Sundays at my suburban church that a few of the more staid, old-time members used to object loudly at every annual meeting. I continued to get my way, but there were some baptismal services where I was careful not to meet their critical eyes. I knew they would be enjoying any miscues. There were plenty.

My worst experience—the one they grinned at most—was the Sunday I had sixteen babies and toddlers to deal with at the large font just below the pulpit. One tot tried to make a break for the door during the preliminary prayers and was only stopped by his father's flying tackle. This hot pursuit ended in a wailing that made all the others sit up and get restive.

I had decided to begin with the older ones and work my way down to the infants-in-arms. It was a fundamental error. As the first three- or four-year-old was led forward, I could tell by the look in his eyes he thought I was up to no good. When I picked him up and tried to splash water on his forehead, his doubts turned to certainty. He writhed, he cried, and he delivered some very energetic kicks. The message was not lost on the others. They started to cry as soon as their parents headed towards my robed figure at the front. Each outdid the other. It was rather difficult to maintain full Anglican dignity.

By the time all sixteen were baptized I had more water on my surplice than in the font. My stole was hanging askew and the look of professional sweetness one was supposed to wear felt less sincere.

That was a while ago. Today the churches are taking a much stricter line. Some of them defend it as tough love or "taking our theology more seriously." Whatever the justification, it is a mistake. To turn people away or take a power trip at their expense is to miss the opportunity to serve.

The Church was never meant to be some kind of exclusive, élitist club. Its true nature is to be the one institution or community that exists for the sake of those who don't belong.

Misusing the Bible

Homosexuality, abortion, "test-tube" babies—when it comes to these kinds of ethical debates there are really three groups of people. There are those who prefer to ignore them completely in the hope that they'll go away. There are those who arrive at firm, well-thought-out positions and who yet remain open to fresh argument or evidence. And then there are those whose minds are made up and closed as tightly as a steel trap-door. They see the world in two tones only: black and white.

The problem with this last group is that too often they take refuge behind the phrase "The Bible says . . . ." Such a formula is intended to end all further speculation or reasoning.

It's not that the Bible is not important, even an ultimate in my own moral thinking or that of countless millions; it's just that it can and does "say" many things. If you are arbitrary and selective enough you can make it say almost anything you please.

Historically the Bible has been misused and misquoted to justify all forms of outrage against humanity—from burning heretics and witches to all-out "holy" war. And it is still going on. For example, a racial timebomb wouldn't be ticking away in South Africa today if some Afrikaaner theologians had not provided apartheid with a biblical grounding. The "separate development of races" is rooted in a warped reading of verses twisted out of holy scripture. One of the most blatant instances of using the Bible unfairly and harshly to bolster one's case can be seen in the current discussion of AIDS. According to some of the more

rigidly righteous, AIDS is proof of God's "hatred" of, and judgment upon, homosexual acts. As one pastor put it, seeking a
cure for the disease would be a waste of millions of dollars. The
real cure? A simple return to what the Bible says. How anyone
can hold such a cruel, vengeful view of God and still want to
be known as Christian is beyond me.

This aside, the question of what the Bible "says" about homosexuals is by no means as simple as the quoters of verses about
Sodom and Gomorrah would have us think. In truth, nearly
every major church commission of the past twenty-five years
has found, upon examining the various passages, that they do
not support the traditional condemnatory attitude of the Judeo-
Christian ethic.

There are explicit prohibitions in the Bible against sexual acts
with those of one's own gender. But, as many moral theologians
now argue, seen in their own historical context and in the light
of our new knowledge, these call for fresh insight. Thus the
United Church task force of two years ago said: "Our basic conclusion is that these passages do not *and cannot* [my italics] provide the church with specific guidance about homosexuality and
the place of gay and lesbian Christians in the church."

In a study commissioned by the Catholic Theological Society
of America, *Human Sexuality: New Directions in American Catholic
Thought*, we read: " . . . where there is sincere affection, responsibility, and the germ of authentic human relationship—in other
words, where there is love—God is surely present."

In part, the taboo against homosexuality in the Hebrew Bible
was based upon a fear of any sexual bonding that could lead
to a decline in the numerical strength of the tribe or nation. But,
as anyone who reads the relevant parts of both Old and New
Testaments discovers, the deep, overwhelming concern is not
about sex, but about idolatry. In the ancient culture surrounding
both the Jews and the early Christians, sex with male or female
prostitutes was part of all fertility-type cults. To be one with the
temple prostitutes was to be one with the cult's god(s). Abhorr-
ence of idolatry spilled over to anything remotely connected
with it.

One other most significant factor must be taken into account.
The biblical writers—for example, St. Paul in Romans 1:26-32—
are talking about homosexual acts deliberately chosen and done
for cheap thrills by those who have tried every other sexual

pleasure. Nowhere is anything said about the constitutive homosexual, the vast majority of gay people who no more chose to be "that way" than I chose to have blue eyes.

Thus to demand celibacy from those clergy and members of every Protestant denomination who cannot help being gay, while heterosexuals are under no such constraint, seems unjust and hypocritical. Most progressive thinkers today, Protestant, Anglican, and Roman Catholic, would agree with Gregory Baum's 1974 statement in his article "Catholic Homosexuals" (*Commonweal*, vol. 99): "If it is true that some people are constitutively homosexual and that homosexual relations allow for mutuality, then, from the viewpoint of Christian theology, it is the task of homosexuals to acknowledge themselves as such before God, accept their sexual inclination as their calling, and explore the meaning of this inclination for the Christian life."

The Crisis in Organized Religion

I was struck by the wording of a report on a recent Gallup Poll, headlined, ''87 percent of Canadians believe in God and Heaven.'' The article began with an almost triumphal ring: "God is alive and well and living in heaven, most Canadians believe"—as though it were the reassurance the Creator has been anxiously waiting to hear.

It reminded me of the story told by a Polish-born professor I once had. He said that long ago, in the village he was brought up in, there was a furious ''God debate'' among the two hundred and fifty inhabitants. They argued the question of God's existence in the streets, in the shops, and in the assembly hall. When finally they decided to have a referendum, God won out by one vote!

Yet, even though it cannot have surprised God, the news that nearly 90 percent of the population here believes in God and the afterlife should give religious leaders cause for alarm. The reason? A Gallup poll on church attendance issued a few weeks ago bore this headline: "Record low 32 percent go to church (synagogue, etc.)."

Roman Catholic officials and observers were said to have been most stunned by the report because, even with the 1985 papal visit to Canada, there has been a large decline in the numbers going to weekly (mandatory) mass. In 1957, 87 percent of Catholics went regularly to church. The latest poll indicates that just 43 percent go today. My reluctant prediction for all religious bodies in Canada is that this situation will get much worse, especially if economic "good times" return. We lag about fifteen to twenty years behind Europe in these matters. In England less than 10 percent of Anglicans go to church, and they are closing roughly ninety churches a year.

The point is that if the vast majority of people believe two of the most cardinal teachings of religion, yet avoid active participation in the rites and obligations of worship almost three to one, organized religion is facing a real crisis. Any business or sport would take immediate steps to see what was wrong and put it right—imagine Harold Ballard with less than one-third of the seats at his Maple Leaf Gardens "temple" to hockey filled for a game. If even some of the energy now directed into fighting for or against choice in abortion, or the funding of separate schools, or a dozen other controversial matters, were to be focused on why so many "believers" find church irrelevant to basic living, some answers might be found.

However, for those who articulately speak out against religious faith on the premise that this is the stuff of wish-fulfilment, irrationality, or a simple unwillingness to move into the age of science and technology, the poll has its surprises too. Are we to conclude that 87 percent of Canadian adults are simply superstitious, naive, misled, or completely untouched by the scientific method? Are such beliefs—as a number of recent letters I've received claim—some soon-to-be-discarded vestiges of a previous evolutionary stage in our development? Or, since people as they grow older tend to become even firmer in their belief in an afterlife, are we looking at the projection of a naked fear of dying—one more insurance policy just in case? I don't believe so.

One of the regrettable features of the current scene is the revival of a once-settled feud between science and religion in the pseudo-battle between ''creationists'' and those who endorse some form of the theory of evolution. The vast majority of believers rightly see no contradiction in holding both views together. To me, it is far more marvellous and intellectually compelling to believe the creator took untold millions of years to bring humans gradually into being than to take the Genesis myth literally and hold that we were "zapped" from the mud in an instant.

There need be no quarrel between religious "knowing" and scientific "knowing." In fact, science needs, and leaps forward by means of, intuitive or imaginative insights and hunches. This was as true of old Archimedes in his bathtub shouting, "Eureka!," as it was of Isaac Newton under the apple tree, or of Albert Einstein in our own era.

Similarly, the leap of faith for religion is based upon a rational foundation. The Judeo-Christian tradition insists on loving God with "all your mind" as well as heart. When the "leap" occurs of trusting where you can not "prove," it is, as with the scientists, not *irrational*, against reason, but *nonrational*—just a different *way* of knowing.

Humanity has always known there is a Creator-Spirit or God. It has always known this life is a doorway to a larger reality. It knows this the same way you or I know a human tear means something more than a certain amount of saline solution secreted by the lachrymal gland in response to certain stimuli.

To have full knowledge of tears—or of love, or anything that ultimately matters—you need more than the evidence of the senses and of what can be measured or predicted scientifically. You need the knowledge of the heart; you need poets, artists, mystics, saints—of all those who have "reasons reason knows not of."

Apocalypse Now?

We are daily bombarded with so much sheer nonsense that most of us have learned how, with a little bit of luck, to ignore it. There is also, however, *dangerous* nonsense, which we ignore at our peril. I am thinking particularly of the growing belief that Armageddon—a nuclear confrontation in which God will intervene to end this age—is just around the corner; that this is part of God's plan of salvation for the elect; and that all the details for the end are laid out in the Bible.

According to the June 1986 issue of the *United Church Observer*, a U.S. poll showed that 39 percent of respondents believed the biblical reference to Armageddon is a prophecy about nuclear war.

Some 20 million copies of Hal Lindsey's *The Late Great Planet Earth* have now been sold. In it he elaborates, in a sensationalistic, highly subjective style, the fundamentalist thesis that God is about to wrap up history; the second coming is at hand. Like the countless others down the ages who have trumpeted the imminence of doom for the wicked and a thousand-year reign of bliss for the saved, Lindsey and his cohorts have mined anew the motherlode of all such speculations: the Book of Daniel and the Revelation of St. John the Divine. Taking the vivid symbolism and verses that unquestionably refer not to the twentieth century but to the trials and tribulations of those believers for whom these books were written some two millennia ago, the literalists forcibly fit them into a blueprint for our own times.

While the rest of us are upset or confused by world famines, natural disasters, terrorism, alleged declines in faith or morals, and the various threats to the planet from pollution, energy depletion, overpopulation, and the bomb, the self-styled "saved" can afford to be smug. After all, "it's in the book" anyway. What's more, the scenario calls for them to be ''raptured''—caught up into Jesus' arms in the sky—before the nuclear explosions start. That is the whole point of the bornagainer's bumper sticker: "In the event of the rapture, the driver of this car will disappear."

What makes so many gullible enough to swallow all this is their enormous longing for absolute answers, which the Armageddon-pushers appear to satisfy. Their predictions gain an aura of plausibility because they dare to find patterns of meaning in the otherwise mind-boggling possibilities before us, today and tomorrow. Are there tornadoes, floods, and famines? They can cite Bible verses to show these are signs of the coming end. Are there wars and "rumors of wars," are there new cults on every side as the mainline churches steadily lose members and water down the faith? These too have been predicted. Similarly with political events such as the establishment of the state of Israel, the rise of Red China, the formation of the Common Market—said to be the Roman Empire renewed—and the Soviet Union's alleged dreams of world domination. Each of these is made to authenticate the timetable for the final apocalypse.

Certainly this kind of preaching makes the average sermon in your average church seem pretty dull by comparison. By saying little about the real nature of the apocalyptic material in the Bible, and little that is helpful to people struggling to keep their faith as the world seems at times to be falling apart, the mainline churches have left the field wide open to the lunatic fringe.

These fundamentalists are not only totally misreading the Bible texts—when they treat them as predictions aimed at today, they are abusing them. Claiming to take the Bible seriously, they are actually prostituting it to their own very arbitrary opinions. They read into it what they want to find, instead of letting it speak for itself.

Perhaps more seriously, all this talk about inevitable wars and then a nuclear Armageddon undermines the nerve of those who should be seeking peace. It creates in the public mind a sense of passive resignation to disasters and the risk of nuclear cataclysm, just when we need a global awakening to sound an overwhelming *no* to this "abomination of desolation."

Worst of all, such a fatalistic and inexorably violent theology provides a justification for the president of the United States and his hawks at the Pentagon to go all out in their risky games. Reagan has kept his own religious beliefs fairly private, but the language and thinking of the Late Great Planet Earth crowd can often be heard in his speeches. He has several times referred to Armageddon as if it were a necessary future event instead of merely a biblical figure of speech to symbolize that evil will eventually be conquered. Moreover, he has uncritically adopted the view of this religious right that the Soviet Union is the source of all terrorism and evil—it is "an evil empire." The corollary of this is that the U.S.S.R. must be destroyed.

That Lindsey and Falwell and their ilk have the ear of their president in an unparalleled, frightening way can be seen in the naive statements Reagan periodically makes about "communist-inspired" terrorism, blaming a list of nations but saying nothing about American terrorism and CIA brutality throughout Central America. The most glowing example is his support for the Contras in Nicaragua.

Most frightening of all, he says nothing about the most horrendous, diabolical form of terrorism in the history of man—the ultimate use of nuclear arms towards which his spiritual advisers now seem bent on propelling him. And in the name of a God of love and mercy!

Drastic Solutions

I don't know anyone in North Dakota, so I was surprised to get a call from there the other day. The woman on the line said she was phoning for her husband, a farmer. Listening to Canadian radio while ploughing, he had heard a commentary I did on religion and terrorism and had left his tractor to ask his wife to get a copy of my column on the same topic.

This is but one example of what has been a remarkable response to both items. The issue is clearly one that has bothered a lot of people for a long time and has been heavily underscored by the extraordinary acts of terrorism in recent years. The nagging question remains, however, of what is to be done about the shadow or demonic side of religion as it unleashes its power in unexpected, sometimes lethal ways.

Some of those who have called or written have a simple, if somewhat drastic, solution. They advocate an end to all religion as speedily as possible. Pointing to world trouble spots—Northern Ireland, Lebanon, India—they argue that if religion could be outlawed or, more slowly, outgrown, a key ingredient in the chemistry of strife would disappear. One cause of hatred and armed conflict would have been dealt with.

There are days when the violence being done in God's name could tempt me to agree with this. But we all know it isn't going to happen. Attempts to end faith by force or edict have never worked. What is now happening in the Soviet Union is a cardinal example; all the sources indicate a massive religious resurgence there, particularly among young adults. In East Germany too, and in many respects in China, church life is more vibrant, more reality-based, than anywhere in the West.

Persecution only serves to strengthen religion. As they said in the first centuries of Christianity, "the blood of the martyrs is the seed of the Church." This resilience of religion, this toughness and ability to endure and ultimately defeat attempts at suppression, is not due to some human perversity or love of superstition, as some would hold. The religious impulse persists because, however warped or even demonic it may become, it witnesses to something fundamental and ineradicable in the human mind and heart. It corresponds to an almost universally perceived reality—however named or worshipped—which we call God.

This "wholly other," which is nevertheless "closer to us than breathing, nearer than hands or feet," does not depend upon Gallup polls or the decline and fall of institutions, rituals, or priestly castes. It is an eternal verity and there will never come a day when at least some people somewhere will not respond in awe, obedience, love.

Most of those I have heard from, however, hold a different view. They feel that, since the major faiths have similar ultimate goals and share the ethical imperative to love God and neighbor, they should come together in one united, global religion that would cull the best insights from each. This idea certainly has its attractions. At first sight it looks very much like the kind of spiritual quantum leap forward many intellectuals believe humanity must take soon if we are not to annihilate ourselves.

But it's not likely to happen. We all know how many sects and denominations lie behind the one name "Christianity." Perhaps we are less aware how similar splitting has affected Islam, Hinduism, Buddhism, and Judaism. None of these is the monolith it may seem to the outsider.

The Anglican Church has two different theological colleges facing each other across a street at the University of Toronto campus. Another warning is the story of how decades of planning for a union between the United Church and the Anglicans self-destructed when it came time to do something besides talk. In fact, my reading of the entire ecumenical movement among Christians worldwide is that it has currently stalled. Don't be fooled by the rhetoric; by now it has become ritualized window-dressing in many ways. In any case, the blending of all denominations and faiths into one homogeneous porridge—a total uniformity of ritual and dogma—would not be desirable even if it were feasible.

There is a glorious splendor in the multiplicity of ways in which we humans approach God, the "beyond in our midst." I, for one, would not like to see the loss of richness that would result from a merger of every Christian body, never mind the loss implied in merging, say, Islam and Judaism.

Once again, the real answer to the role of religion in violence and terrorism today is a meeting of world religious leaders in which they would explore and affirm the central, universal moral consequences of claiming to know and/or love God.

The Depth Dimension

Rulers in ancient times regularly put to death the bearers of bad news. We are, fortunately, less ruthless, but the "kill-the-messenger" syndrome surfaces constantly in criticisms of the mass media today. People need and want scapegoats, and in hard times TV, radio, and press afford broad, convenient targets. As a journalist I frequently find myself having to defend the media both in my classes at the Toronto School of Theology and elsewhere. There is, however, one criticism I find impossible to parry: that in covering the news the media are, deep down, extraordinarily shallow most of the time.

When you combine this superficiality with the illusion, too often given, that to have watched a particular news clip, to have heard a particular radio report, or to have read a specific story is to have been fully informed about the matter, you have a recipe for what can only be called "informed ignorance." I know the usual excuses—lack of time, lack of space, the need for immediacy—but frankly they won't wash. It comes down to rethinking priorities.

For example, there hasn't been a major news story I can remember that does not have a "depth dimension" that can be described as having to do with religion and morals. This is true of the suspected involvement of Sikh extremists in the 1985 sabotage of the Air-India flight, of the TWA hijacking, and of the hostages held by Shiites in Beirut; it is true of the struggle for nuclear sanity; it holds for the entire debate over the economy and unemployment in Canada. The list is virtually endless— from the frontiers of medicine and physics to the probings of outer space, practically every area of controversy and of discovery is loaded with religious and ethical dilemmas. Yet in far too many media hierarchies the religious element is regarded as being of little or no interest, something for the back pages or a cub reporter.

Contrast this treatment with the space and time allocated to sports. I love nearly all forms of sport myself. During ten years of university—I was a slow learner—I competed in basketball, rowing, and English rugger. I like watching hockey, baseball, and the rest. But considering that nothing in the welter of sports, stories about sports, endless TV coverage, endless, tiresome post-mortems of games, etc., makes an iota of difference to anyone's life or destiny, such an obsession is surely out of sync with reality.

I'm obviously not in favor of more coverage of sermons, parish suppers, or the internal affairs of denominations. I'm talking about religion in its widest and most significant application, about that aspect of life which has to do with ultimate questions of meaning, of right and wrong, of what it is to be human.

These kinds of issues are termed "soft" by veteran newspeople riveted on "hard" news. But it is precisely the so-called soft factors here that alone can give all the rest of the news any real sense at all.

For instance, for several years we have been inundated with references to the Shiite Muslims in Iran and Lebanon. Yet how many readers and/or viewers have the foggiest notion of who or what that name implies? How many Canadians know that, almost from its birth, Islam has been split into two major groups, the Sunni and the Shiah Muslims, or that this "fault line" of the human soul is the same as that which divides Christianity into Protestantism and Roman Catholicism, and Buddhism into Mahayana and Hinayana Buddhism? The Shiah faith, like Catholicism, emphasizes the need for charismatic leaders or immams who act as mediators between human and divine, while the Sunni, like Protestantism, holds that the believer stands directly face to face with God.

There is no excuse for terrorism or hijacking, but the events in Lebanon only begin to have some coherence when you know that the Christians (Maronites), although the minority, have been clinging to their wealth and, above all, their political ascendancy with the help of the United States and Israel. The Shiites, who outnumber their Sunni brethren by a considerable margin, have always been at the bottom of the heap in Lebanon—the poorest, the most disadvantaged in every way. Here, then, as in most of the world's trouble spots, we are seeing the backlash effect of justice too long denied, the inevitable revolt of an oppressed people seeking their place in the sun. Fundamentalist Islam sees the U.S. as "an evil empire" or "the Great

Satan'' for almost the identical reasons that fundamentalist-inspired Ronald Reagan sees the Soviets in the same light.

In fact, it daily becomes more obvious that the Pentagon's entire strategy, nuclear and other, cannot be fully comprehended without reference to the apocalyptic ravings of fundamentalists like Hal Lindsey, with his thesis that nuclear war is part of God's plan. In short, there has never been a time when religion played a larger part in human affairs.

Faiths Can Co-exist

JERUSALEM—Dec. 2, 1985. The Middle East—exotic, chaotic, brimming with tensions that disturb the sleep of those who dream of peace, yet filled with ageless symbols of hope. The birthplace of three great world religions: Judaism, Christianity, and Islam. After visiting Israel again—my fourth trip in the region, including wholly Arab countries as well—some impressions leave an indelible mark.

Jerusalem at dawn, with rosy light playing softly from gold and silvered mosques, church towers, and time-hallowed Jewish shrines. The rising sun out of the desert to the east makes the old walled city on top of Mount Zion glow like some rare jewel.

Standing by the Western Wall, all that remains of the famous Second Temple built by Herod the Great, I watch as the pious pray or reach high to stick little scraps of paper holding special requests into the crevices between the square-hewn blocks of stone. The square in front of the wall is roped off to create a synagogue, and several Bar-Mitzvahs are taking place.

At that very moment sounds the Muslim call to prayer from nearby minarets, and loud-pealing bells announcing the hour of Mass. It strikes home powerfully that these three faiths can and do co-exist here, perhaps as nowhere else.

There is harmony, too, in the labyrinthine twistings of the ancient bazaar, in the intermingling of the Muslim-Arab, Christian-Arab, and Jewish stalls, with their glittering array of everything from pastry baked while you watch to oriental rugs or antique jewelry. Nothing is sold at the asking price here—haggling and bartering add spice for buyer and seller alike. The place reeks of authenticity, of an age that makes it almost time-less, at one with every ancient bazaar throughout the east from Istanbul to Marrakesh.

The Sea of Galilee, ringed by bare hills and mountains, includ-ing the Golan Heights to the east, remains one of the most eerily calming spots on the face of the earth. Yet as we stood looking out over it, the whine of jet fighters in mock battle above spoke of other realities. As I read the Sermon on the Mount to a group of Canadians on the low hill where tradition says Jesus first gave it, the radical words "blessed are the peacemakers" were almost lost in the roar of the same planes.

The *Jerusalem Post* today reports that for the 1986 fiscal year Israel is seeking $2.2 billion (U.S.) for arms alone—a 50 percent increase over the 1985 level. The request must be seen against the backdrop of recent large-scale American arms sales to Saudi Arabia and Jordan. But it's like trying to put out a brush fire by throwing gasoline on it. When, you wonder, will this mad-ness cease?

Conditions among Arabs living in the occupied territories of the West Bank confirm the *Post*'s reports that Palestinians in the camps and elsewhere are the hardest hit by the present eco-nomic crisis, with an 800 + percent inflation rate and lack of jobs. That, combined with recent Jewish terrorist attacks on Arabs, could, as one writer says, "politicize middle-class Arabs who up to now have avoided political activism."

In the paper an Arab journalist, critical of the terrorism and the treatment of Arab prisoners in Israeli jails, says it is time the Jews saw his people neither as victims, nor as mad killers, nor as scum to be eradicated: "Israelis and Jews abroad must accept Palestinians as full partners in this land. Both our peoples . . . have a right to live in our land with dignity. Otherwise there will be no peace. And terror will beget more terror." These are wise words, yet it strikes you how free one can be in Israel to say things that in North America would be preposterously labelled "anti-Semitic."

It is popular today to write and talk about Armageddon. The correct way to write the word is Har-Magedon, meaning the "mountains of Meggido." Meggido, the ancient fortress, stood where the mountains meet the vast Plain of Esdraelon, the scene of so many of the bloodiest wars in Hebrew history. In fact, the name eventually came to be synonymous with the classic battleground of scripture.

Naturally, then, it became the symbol for the mythical final battle of all time (Rev. 16:16). But nothing was further from the minds of those who wrote of this ultimate event than the nuclear holocaust possible today. In the Bible we read of a symbolic final war between good and evil in which God triumphs. That scenario is worlds away from a nuclear war in which there would be no discrimination between good and bad, evil or innocent, but a total destruction of all life—a victory for nobody but the devil himself, the final triumph of chaos.

I don't believe in any literal battle of Armageddon planned by a God worthy of the name any more now than when, as a boy attending a tiny Gospel church, I had to listen to the ignorant preaching of a cleric who revelled in gore. Standing near Meggido this week, I realized there is almost as much to fear from those who love announcing a God-willed Armageddon as from any enemy.

To indulge in this lunacy is to risk the self-fulfilment of one's own prophecy. Our task is to work for God's peace, not to preach annihilation. To do this we need no new religious revelations from the Middle East. Rather, we need a renewed understanding of, and commitment to, those we already have.

The Shadow Side of Religion

The 1984 assassination of Indian Prime Minister Indira Gandhi and the continuing cycle of bloody events between Hindus and Sikhs that has followed has much more to do with politics than with religious differences. Yet, as in so many trouble spots around the world, it would be naive not to recognize the part religion has played in making such savagery possible.

This fact alone should provide sobering food for thought to those religious leaders and groups who appear to believe that all you have to do to solve any human dilemma is to aim more religion at it and, hallelujah, you have the solution. This pious hope needs exploding for the myth it is. The last thing Lebanon needs is more religion. The same is true of Iran, Northern Ireland, and a host of other places.

Religion can heal relationships and strengthen families. It can also tear them apart. It can eradicate prejudice and racism. And it can harden them like flint while, as in South Africa, justifying them in the name of God. Religion can cleanse false guilt, worry, and tension. But it can also heap all three on the backs of the faithful.

Religion is a two-edged sword; it has a shadow, demonic side. As Pascal once wrote, people never do evil more cheerfully than when they do it in the name of religion. You don't have to go back to the crusades or the Spanish inquisition for examples. There is plenty of evidence on the contemporary scene, from anti-Catholic hate literature disguised as comic books to the attack on the Golden Temple in Amritsar.

One of the most frightening aspects of the present planet-threatening crisis between the United States and the Soviet Union is the way both sides are committed to what is in reality a Messianic foreign policy. President Ronald Reagan is certain he knows the will of God for humanity, that all the powers of goodness, purity, and truth are on the side of America. The Kremlin bosses are just as convinced that the gods of historical necessity and dialectical materialism make their cause the sole righteous one. They too have their prophets—Marx, Lenin, and the rest. They have their sacred, infallible books, their vision of a "heaven"—the mythical classless society that has eluded communism so far. But the existence of two nuclear titans, each fervently certain that it alone has the answer to humanity's salvation, is the most potent recipe possible for universal destruction.

The dark side of religion's ambiguous nature—its propensity to increase intolerance, to reinforce a false sense of superiority to others who differ, its readiness for violence—cries out for explanation. With all its endless potential for giving meaning, inspiration, values, and ultimate goals, how can this bitterly destructive, demonic side exist?

There are several reasons. Religion deals with those matters that touch us most deeply, that lie at the very foundation of our being. Thus it confronts us where our profoundest emotions flow. Since in the last resort most of us are guided much more by emotion than by reason, it is not surprising that our darker impulses often invoke God's blessing.

Then, too, however much religion may be based upon divine

revelation, whether contemporary or coded in ancient scriptures, it is very much a product of human hands and minds. The differing groups within Judaism, Christianity, Islam, or Buddhism show that you can take the same revelation and respond to it in dozens of ways. What people have done with the original teachings of the great world religions often bears little resemblance to what the founders themselves seem to have had in mind. Since there is human input, it follows necessarily there will be human error as well.

Some will argue that their religion is a direct gift from God. But like all such gifts—freedom, sex, food, wine—it still has a shadow side. As the ancients said, *corruptio optimi pessima*—the perversion of the best is the worst. It is an unwritten law that evil mounts on the shoulders of the good. Yet to say this is by no means to put down religion, nor is it to advocate pessimism about all human ideals. Quite the contrary.

It is, rather, an urgent plea for some honesty, humility, humor, and, above all, some real self-knowledge on the part of all religions as they brandish their warnings, disciplines, dogmas, and solutions in the face of today's complexities. When religious leaders of all persuasions call for an end to oppression or injustices, it would lend credibility if at the same time they publicly confessed the way their own religions have contributed to these very evils. In the prescriptions for peace and disarmament it would be reassuring to hear some word of repentance for religion's role in wars both past and present. If they speak of their religion as though it alone held the panacea for global unity and human solidarity, we need to hear from their lips some acknowledgment that their own disunity goes far to negate their claims.

As Dietrich Bonhoeffer said, religion has caused so much harm, it needs to "earn the right" to address the world anew. People are looking for the reality of lives lived, not of words spoken, no matter how eloquent.

Anti-Semitism and Christianity

Adolf Hitler had some stunning words for two German bishops who came to see him in 1940 to remonstrate with him over his treatment of Jews. He said: "I am only putting into practice

what you Christians have been teaching for 2000 years." Hitler
was a liar and this statement was a gross distortion. But it held
a horrific truth at its core. Without nearly 2000 years of officially-
taught Christian contempt for Judaism and its people, the atroc-
ities of the Holocaust could never have taken place.

Since 1945, Church leaders of all denominations have made
powerful statements against the evil of anti-Semitism. Christian
scholars have patiently and frankly examined both the New Testament writings and Church history for anti-Jewish bias and
prejudice. Their findings have been published. And their conclusions have been unanimous: read in an uneducated fashion,
the Gospels, especially Matthew and John, can be used to foster
anti-Jewish attitudes and feelings; what's more, the official
pronouncements of the Church, down the centuries, exhibit a
frightening intolerance towards "God's Chosen People."

Before saying more, it is important to point out that, although
Church leadership has done its best to face this dark side of the
Christian past, the full dimensions of the matter have never
fully leaped across the gulf between pulpit and pew. Ordinary
rank-and-file Christians, never mind the majority of the world's
people who have no more than a nodding acquaintance with
the faith, have no idea of any Christian complicity in the
Holocaust.

That is at least part of the reason why even the grisly accounts
of the death camps now coming out of the trial of John Demjan-
juk in Israel—at stake is whether the retired Cleveland auto-
worker is none other than "Ivan the Terrible," a bestial guard
at the Treblinka incinerators—seem somehow remote and unreal
to many. Similarly, while most applaud the recent call by Mr.
Justice Jules Deschênes for a made-in-Canada prosecution of
suspected Nazi war criminals living here (though we may wonder why it took over forty years to make such a move), there
is again a general sense that this has little to do with any of us
personally.

One of the central thrusts of modern study of the Bible is how
the life situation of the early Christians conditioned the way
they told the story of Jesus. We can see in the Gospels the reflec-
tion of the tensions and strains between the newly emerging
faith and its Jewish parent.

The Gospels were not written primarily as history, but as
statements of faith aimed at various groups of believers. They

were to be used in catechizing, in worship, and in conflicts with critics. As the great Roman Catholic New Testament scholar Raymond Brown has written, "The Word of God comes to us in the words of men."

The Gospels were written some decades after the events they describe were recorded. They set what was said and done at the *beginning* of the first century by Jesus in the context of the world of the *late* first century.

Moreover, they were composed at a time of great hostility between Christians and the Pharisee-led synagogue. Thus words spoken by Jesus when he and his followers represented simply one of many sects within Judaism were used as weapons by an increasingly non-Jewish church, and their tone changed completely. When Matthew and John speak disparagingly of "the Jews," they are writing as Jews themselves about the collaborationist Jewish sect, the Sadduccees, who plotted with the Romans to put Jesus to death.

Because the early Christians had to make their way in a Roman-dominated empire—at a time when their Jewish rivals were out of favor because of revolts—you can see in the New Testament a clear tendency to exaggerate Jewish blame for the Crucifixion and play down the Roman. The historical reality is that only Rome had the power to execute anyone in the Judea of Jesus' time. What is more, death on a cross is a Roman form of execution. If Jesus had been guilty of blasphemy (it was not blasphemy to claim to be Messiah) the Jewish penalty would have been stoning.

Tragically, the story of Jesus' death, read out of context, has been used down the ages as justification for all kinds of vituperation and violence against Jews. Down into the modern era, it was common in parts of Europe for Christians to rush out, after hearing the Passion stories read in church during Holy Week, to pounce on passing Jews and beat them as "Christ-killers."

In fact, the word anti-Semitism is the creation of nineteenth-century scientists in Germany concerned with bogus racial theories. Thus the more accurate way to describe this centuries-old Christian contempt is anti-Judaism. Most Christians, let alone outsiders, are unaware that official Church positions *vis-à-vis* Judaism, especially from the time of the marriage of Church and state, with Constantine's conversion in the fourth century, down to the collapse of the Holy Roman Empire, prefigured nearly all the discrimination practiced by the Nazis—short of the "Final Solution." The Nazis were the very opposite of Christian, but their policies toward Jews fulfilled the ultimate logic of Christian anti-Jewish myths.

Christianity began as a sect of Judaism; Jesus was Jewish and so were his first disciples. But the Jewish people as a whole rejected the, to them, abhorrent idea of a Messiah who dies on a Roman cross. The emerging Church thus had a serious problem. If Jesus was the promised Messiah, why didn't "God's people" accept him? The answer, worked out in haste and in the bitter anger of a "family quarrel," was to be the source of untold tragedies over the centuries.

Adherents to the newly-born faith proceeded to define their own identity by negating and ridiculing the faith of what they now called the "Old" Testament and its people. The early Church fathers heaped abuse and distortion upon the beliefs and practices of the rival synagogue. Jews were said to be blind, carnal, perfidious, a people with a history of unspeakable crimes culminating in deicide—surely a contradiction in terms if there ever was one!

St. John Chrysostom (the name means "golden-mouth"), the most eloquent preacher of the late fourth century (A.D. 347–407), would be properly jeered today, and then tried and jailed, if he were to utter half of what he used to claim against Jews. His writings are full of unbelievable abuse. Judaism, he says, is not just obsolete but cursed. He rants on about the synagogue as a den of thieves and harlots. There is no limit to his hate and rage: "It is because you killed Christ. It is because you stretched out your hand against the Lord . . . that there is now no restoration, no mercy anymore and no defense." Add rhetoric like this to the mix whenever the mob is looking for a scapegoat, and violence is certain to result. And Chrysostom was only one in a long succession of such hate-mongering "spiritual" leaders.

From these early polemics and a false reading of the scriptures behind them, all the deadly later myths were built: for example, the so-called blood libel, which was resurrected by Nazis but was in vogue in the Middle Ages. It alleged that Jews murdered Christian babies to get blood for Passover and other rites. Jews were even held to be the cause of the Black Death, allegedly poisoning the wells of Europe. Jews were routinely denied full rights as citizens, limited to marginal occupations, made to wear the yellow patch or other distinctive clothing, confined to ghettos, forbidden to intermarry with Christians, forced to undergo baptism, and to suffer regular—even if officially frowned-upon—massacres and pogroms, all in the name of God's Church.

Martin Luther, the great Protestant reformer of the sixteenth century, was responsible for some of the most hate-filled insults and slurs against Jews ever written. When he says, "We are at fault for not slaying them," it is not hard to see why Hitler could say he was only putting into practice what Christians had long taught.

It is significant that even Dietrich Bonhoeffer, himself a martyr of the resistance against Hitler and a seminal thinker for modern Christianity, could write in 1934 that the Jews should never be expelled from Europe. They must remain, he said, as a negative witness to Christ, the recipients and exemplification of Divine wrath! As Rosemary Ruether has written, in *Faith and Fratricide*, "He is oblivious to the fact that it is this very myth that lies behind the history that helped shape anti-Semitism."

Coming to grips with the Holocaust may be an impossible task, however many war criminals are brought to trial. It is not made easier by wishful thinking that avoids facing the gross unpleasantness of Christian complicity.

Bias and the Bible

I seldom listen to or watch religious programs unless I have to. The "I have the Ultimate Mystery in my pocket" syndrome smacks of spiritual pornography; even Billy Graham, for all his integrity, falls into this trap. But programs *about* religion are another matter. They can be fascinating.

The reason is that religion, in spite of current distortions, deals with the issues that ultimately matter most to us, whether we are "believers" or not. It is to religion that the deepest questions belong—meaning, right and wrong, the origins and destiny of humanity, life and death. This is why I have no patience with those who blandly pontificate about how one should avoid the subjects of religion, politics, or sex in polite conversation.

What other topic is there but sports or the weather if you avoid the Big Three? In fact, since religion really includes politics and sex anyway, one could argue that it is the only worthwhile topic, period.

There was a TV show one night dealing with the question of whether or not the Vatican has too much power over its flock. It underlined a fundamental difficulty plaguing Christianity and other world faiths as we get closer to A.D. 2000. The program revolved around three experts—an Anglican, a Lutheran, and a Roman Catholic—who each soon made it evident that his own group's view of religion was the right one and all others were, if not perverse, then certainly inferior.

The Lutheran, a professor from the Missouri Synod, the smallest and most conservative branch of Lutheranism, was the most blatant in his claims to a monopoly on truth. According to him, the reason there are so many different brands of Christianity is that all the others read their own interpretations into the Bible. His group alone simply allows the Bible to "speak for itself." In his view the Bible is an exceedingly simple collection of writings. When you read it "objectively," its truth passes straight into your mind and heart with no human additions, interpretations, or subjective coloring. When confronted with the possibility that his group also might have its own slant or selectivity in reading the Bible, he vehemently denied it.

This is a fatal tunnel vision: the inability or unwillingness to face the fact that no matter what claims are made about any sacred writing being the Word of God—Jewish, Christian, Islamic, Buddhist, or Hindu—the scripture itself comes to us in the words of *human* language. As such it is open to, in fact demands, interpretation. This means that subjectivity, bias if you like, is unavoidable. It is part of the human condition. We bring ourselves, our needs, our prejudices, our hopes to everything we do—to writing a column, to understanding any book, however holy.

You'd think this alone would bring a sense of humility and tolerance to all faiths, never mind the fact that they all claim to teach the essential unity and equality of humankind under God. Sadly, it doesn't. In the case of Christians, the claim of any church to be the only true Church, the only one to truly understand the Bible, seems palpably ridiculous.

For example, Jesus spoke only Aramaic. His sayings were

remembered by Aramaic-speakers and only later translated into Greek in what came to be known as the New Testament. Most of us, however, read all this in an English or French translation. We are already twice removed from the original. And at each stage of translation more sifting and changing occur.

Thus while Jesus talks about himself as the Son of Man and preaches the Kingdom of God, Paul knows that the first term makes nonsense in Greek and the other wouldn't be understood by his audience anyway. So he avoids both of them almost entirely. In fact, by comparing the Gospels themselves, scholars can see how even in the earliest handing down of the Jesus tradition there were constant changes, adaptations, and interpretations going on. The theology of Luke is different from Matthew's; Mark's concerns and slants are vastly different from John's. Each sees the Christ-event from his own unique perspective. Each faces an audience with different problems and writes accordingly.

Change and the Catholic Church

Invincible ignorance? In the wake of the controversies surrounding the recent visit of Pope John Paul to the U.S., I am tempted to believe there really is such a thing. There actually are people who adamantly refuse to let their opinions be confused by confrontation with fact.

This was particularly obvious in the discussion carried by CBC Radio's open-line show "Cross Country Checkup" on the last day of the Pope's September 1987 tour. The question put to the national audience was: "Should the Pope be more flexible?"

Now, it is one thing to defend the Pope's unflinching stand on everything from the ban on contraception to the condemnation of homosexual acts as mortal sin—as many of the callers and the prime guest, Anne Roche Muggeridge, vigorously did. I have no problem with that.

What was literally astounding, however, to anyone with the least acquaintance with the history of the Roman Catholic Church, was the repeated insistence that the Pope's rigidity arises from the fact that he has no choice. Authentic Catholic teaching on these matters, we were told, does not change because it cannot. Moreover, what was said and/or implied time and again, both by Muggeridge and by a large number of callers—even one or two who said they were atheists—was that Catholic doctrine has remained unchanged since the time of the early Church.

Unfortunately, this comforting supposition is totally refuted— not by opinion or conjecture, but by the actual record of contradictions and changes in the Church's teaching over nearly two millennia.

As a matter of fact, the major reason why the Roman Catholic Church remains the oldest institution surviving from antiquity is not that it has been rigid or unwilling to adapt, but precisely that it has always managed to change and to "baptize" alien cultures and ideas.

It took the Roman Catholic Church over 1400 years to come to terms with the fact that its authentic teaching on slavery was dead wrong. In fact, as Fr. John Maxwell shows in his book *Slavery and the Catholic Church*, it was not until 1965, at Vatican II, that "the common Catholic teaching concerning the moral legitimacy of the institution of slavery was corrected."

Similarly, anyone who thinks that the Catholic Church has always believed in religious liberty for non-Catholics ought to read about the persecution earlier in this century of Fr. John Courtney Murray for espousing such a view. He was hounded just as Hans Küng and Charles Curran are today. Yet at Vatican II (1962-65) Murray's ideas were vindicated and for the first time Rome officially said that other faiths have a right to religious freedom. As Catholic theologian Fr. Walter Principe has noted, "The magnitude of the change is clear from the strong opposition mounted against its acceptance during the Council."

The same reality appears when you examine the history of Vatican pronouncements and teaching concerning the Jewish people—referred to in Church prayers as late as 1960 as "the perfidious Jews." The changes here, thank God, have been momentous.

In the most recent issue of the Roman Catholic journal *The Ecumenist* (vol. 25, no. 5) in an article entitled "When 'Authentic' Teachings Change," Principe, who is professor of historical theology at St. Michael's College, in Toronto, lists a whole range of important changes in doctrine over the centuries. Among the examples he gives are the following:

• In 1950 Pope Pius XII declared in *Humani Generis* that theologians must teach monogenism, i.e., that mankind had an original single set of parents, since it was hard to square anything else with the Church's teaching on the transmission of original sin. The teaching of this encyclical was soon quietly dropped.

- Whereas earlier this century the removal of a fetus stuck in the Fallopian tubes (known as an ectopic pregnancy) was considered abortion by the Church, some theologians argued against this view, "and their opinions prevailed so that such removal is no longer questioned."

- Regarding marriage, "there have been a number of changes in what was formerly authentic . . . teaching." Pope Gregory I (A.D. 590–604) said that if there was any pleasure involved in the act of intercourse, "married couples break the laws of marriage, befouling their intercourse with their pleasure." Gregory also taught that couples should not receive Holy Communion after marital intercourse. Luckily for Catholics, the Church eventually dropped its allegiance to his views.

- Finally, at Vatican II traditional authentic teaching again was changed when the insistence on the procreation and education of children was no longer insisted on as the primary end of marriage.

III

THE HORMONE ISSUES

Women in the Church

There was a time not long ago when a clergyman could face a congregation largely made up of females and address them as "dearly beloved brethren" without so much as a qualm or blush. But not any more. A revolution is taking place. Women members of every Christian denomination around the world are now pushing, pleading, demanding that ecclesiastical sexism come to an end. They want the equality that a male-dominated institution has been talking about for almost 2000 years while denying its application to more than 50 percent of the population.

That's the context in which the guidelines issued by the General Council of the United Church in August, 1986, have to be viewed. The top decision-making body of Canada's largest Protestant church ruled that, among other things, immediate steps must be taken to widen the use of concepts, metaphors, and other imagery or symbolism that speak of God in female terms, and adopt and use language in worship and Church documents that is inclusive of both males and females.

The new guidelines point out that there are plenty of female images for God in the Bible. The reason there are not more is that Christianity, like Judaism and Islam, emerged in a fiercely patriarchal society. The reason the femaleness that is there—in Jesus' parable of the lost coin (Luke 15), in Old Testament images of God as mother to the Children of Israel—has not been recognized is that until very recently priestly and ministerial castes have been totally male. Men have had a vested interest in keeping things their way.

Nobody at the Sudbury meetings was suggesting the Lord's Prayer, for example, be changed to say, "Our Mother who art in heaven.'' There is no intention of rewriting the Bible to

remove all the exclusive language used by successive generations of male translators. Wherever possible, though, the
Church will now use inclusive words such as person or people
for man; instead of always referring to God as King, Father, He,
or Him, the guidelines call for the inclusive terms God, Father-
Mother, Creator, and Friend.

Some of the delegates in Sudbury were angry at the proposed changes; at the grassroots or congregational level there
has been considerable unrest as well. One is reminded of the
furor caused in the Vatican over the comment of Pope John
Paul I that it is sometimes appropriate to "speak of God also
as our Mother." Nobody knows what striking changes there
might have been in the Roman Catholic Church's attitude to
women if he had lived longer. Because this is not a trivial matter. As anyone who knows anything about the fight against
racism, for instance, realizes, imagery and language have terrible power to oppress and hurt. Stereotype or label some
group and it's easier to keep them down; call the enemy a
disparaging nickname and you can literally do what you like
to them and theirs.

Shortly before the United Church issued its guidelines, a
radical report linking some church attitudes, traditions, and
language to violence against women was approved by the
Anglican Church of Canada. Like their United counterparts,
the Anglicans have recognized that the Church is the strongest
remaining bastion of male chauvinism. Significantly, both
these churches have fully ordained women in their ranks—the
Anglicans for ten years, the United almost since the Church
was launched in 1925. But admitting women to the pulpit or
at the altar is not the same thing as full equality for women
in the Church.

Meanwhile, in England the Church of England still bans
women priests and there is bitter opposition to the idea of
women bishops in any branch of Anglicanism abroad. The
Roman Catholic and Eastern Orthodox Churches, of course,
are still decades away from ordaining women. But it will come.
The Canadian Catholic Bishops are leading the way in the
attempt to find an equal role for women and the elimination
of sexist language from the liturgy at Mass. History will one-
day record the present struggle to emancipate women in
the Church and to feminize our understanding of God as the

most potent phenomenon in the entire development of Christianity.

The recognition of women as full equals is essential for justice. Seeing the nurturing, tender, feminine aspects of the deity is necessary for peace and a non-exploitative relationship with our planet. Worship of a macho, aggressive, punitive male God has too often already condoned our wars and justified the ruin of our mother earth.

Violence Against Women

There are a number of shocking stories of violence against women in the Bible. The worst, and least well-known, occurs in a terrifyingly detailed account in Judges 19. In brief, the narrative deals with a Levite whose concubine—a virtual sex-slave—has run away and gone home to her father. The Levite follows her, finds her, and they are travelling back when night overtakes them. They are about to sleep in a city street, but an old man sees their plight and offers them shelter.

Some of the men of the city then gathered outside and demanded that the Levite be given up to them for homosexual rape. The old man roundly condemned them for this and offered them instead his own virgin daughter and the concubine. "Ravish them," he said, "and do with them what seemeth good to you; but unto this man do not so vile a thing." Here, as elsewhere in the Bible (see Genesis 19), the point is that violence against men is far more serious than that against women.

The mob then took the young girl—promptly handed over by the Levite—and "they knew her and abused her all night until the morning." When this pitiless gang-rape ended, she collapsed near-dead, clutching at the door of the old man's house. Early next day she was discovered there by her master as he was preparing to leave. He issued a curt order to the unconscious victim to get up and join him on the journey, but "none answered." Then he slung her over his donkey, "rose up and gat him to his place."

Somewhere along the road she died, unwept for, untended, truly alone. But the horrors were not over. When he got home, the man "took a knife and laid hold on his concubine, and divided her, together with her bones, into twelve pieces, and sent her into all the coasts of Israel." The passage makes no judgments about the horrendous crime as far as the woman herself is concerned.

As Christian feminist Joyce Holliday wrote in *Sojourners* (June, 1986): "Such unspeakable violence is only possible in a culture in which women have been so objectified as to be considered less than human." To be objectified means to be made an object, a thing, a piece of property and little more.

That's why I thank God one Canadian church is challenging its members and those of other denominations and faiths to look at the tragic contribution of bad religion to violence against women. A radical report, approved now for study by the Anglican Church, says correctly that, for many battered women, their experience of violence at the hands of men is comparable to the societal and physical violence experienced by women in the Bible.

This finding squarely faces the fact that while the story in Judges is an extreme, the Bible, written entirely by men and for nearly 2000 years interpreted always by males, can be and has been used to justify the grossest of violations against the rights and humanity of one-half of the race. Wrongly interpreted by divines and scholars who should have known better, it has even been used to trace the origin of evil itself to women; after all, in this sexist view it was Eve who first succumbed to temptation. Verses in the New Testament about wives keeping themselves in submission to their husbands have been used historically—and still are today by some religionists—to justify men in physically punishing their spouses for real or imagined wrongdoing.

The Anglican study notes, with startling honesty, that wife-beating sometimes occurs today in clergy homes. It calls for a re-examination of church attitudes, traditions, and language to hunt down dehumanizing views of women. Most Rev. Michael Peers, the new primate, has said this could mean, among other things, a change in the wedding service: "The tradition of the father of the bride giving the bride away is rooted in a view of women as property . . . transferring property from father to husband."

Clearly an apology is owed to the women of the world by nearly all organized religions—not just for the horror stories throughout history, but for much of the ongoing discrimination and cultural, if not always physical, violence against them today.

Homosexuality

Like most people, I don't like to think I'm one who gives in easily to panic. But I lost my car in the vast, labyrinthine parking complex under the city's center the other day just when I needed it urgently to get to an appointment. The entire parking lot seemed to be in on a conspiracy to keep me there—like Orpheus in the underworld—wandering endlessly up prison-like stairways and down ramps reeking of oil. And all in vain.

The problem was not so much that I had forgotten to note the floor and section numbers. What had me foxed was that the whole set-up was color-coded . "Just remember your floor color and follow the wide band of it to your section," several signs said. I had told myself that would be easy. I was on the red floor. However, there was an orange floor as well, and I might have been on that. Given the shades of orange and red used there, I couldn't tell them apart.

You see, I'm color-blind. I first discovered it in kindergarten when I crayoned a robin's breast brown and was told off. I always consulted a little girl with straight-slashed bangs, who sat next to me, whenever we were given further coloring to do. Yes, I do see various colors around me. I just can't put the right name to most of them, especially reds and greens. My wife has to check me over whenever I'm going to be in the public eye because my idea of what matches has produced some startling effects at times. And when I worked Saturdays in Eaton's young-men's department, while I was at high school, I used to dread being asked to find pants I thought would go with this or that color of jacket. Some customers would look at my suggested offerings with genuine alarm.

Apart from keeping me from being a first-class bird-watcher, though, this minor disability has caused me little real harm. I mention it here because of one thing: I didn't choose to become color-blind; I can't remember a time when I wasn't; it's an incurable condition. For me it's a given, a part of the way I am and how I see the world.

For the vast majority of the general population it's the very same with their sexual orientation. It's fine, for example, to feel glad that one is attracted to the opposite sex. But nobody I know goes around taking credit for or pride in having consciously chosen to be heterosexual.

As a clergyman who often shared the most intimate details of people's lives, I became aware early that in every congregation—as elsewhere—there are always those whose orientation sexually is towards members of the same sex. They are homosexuals, which, in its Greek root, means just that: attracted to the same sex.

As a journalist I soon realized that there are homosexuals in the clergy as well—sometimes a higher percentage than in some other professions, though there are homosexual doctors, lawyers, architects, and so on, too. I have heard some of their stories, in confidence, first hand. I have read their letters when distance or discretion or fear made such a medium the obvious choice. I have become aware of their agony, self-doubt, and self-accusation as they have wrestled with traditional church teachings and dread of being "found out." In every case I know, the homosexuality was constitutive—part of the person's entire self-awareness. Efforts by themselves or others to change this had only led to further despair, and in some cases to desperate acts.

What is profoundly tragic is the way society still persecutes and discriminates against those who are homosexual, and the way people rally around anti-homosexual myths whenever there is a move to give them their basic human rights. As of this writing (November, 1986) the Liberal cabinet of Ontario is still dragging its feet on passing an amendment to the province's Human Rights Code prohibiting discrimination on the grounds of a person's sexual orientation. Behind the delay is a strange coalition—Catholic bishops and conservative Protestants—who base their protest on three of the worst homophobic myths: that homosexuals pose a threat to family life (if the family is in danger, surely it is the heterosexual majority who are responsible); that they are a menace to children; and that they cannot live a truly Christian life.

The latter myth came to the fore in the spring of 1986 with a homosexual couple's open letter, to the *Presbyterian Record*, challenging their church's official stand that homosexual relationships are sinful. The pair—one of them is ordained and the other preparing "for such service"—said they didn't feel their life together was wrong, and that they were speaking up for "that silent number" in the Church who are both homosexual and "active in leadership." They said they didn't wish to hide their relationship but were forced to "live in a false hypocrisy" by their church.

Today, in fact, all the churches are struggling with what it means to be a homosexual Christian. It was the issue behind the controversial firings of staff at a large Roman Catholic seminary some months earlier. It was at stake in Archbishop L.S. Garnsworthy's suspension of two lesbian deacons who had told their parish they were "married" and expecting a baby. Garnsworthy cited the Anglican bishops' ruling that clergy may be homosexual, but they must not express their sexuality, i.e., must remain celibate. Rome's position is similar.

I leave it to others to judge whether it is realistic or fair to demand celibacy of some when it is not required of other clergy. (Interestingly, when I did a piece on the way some Catholic priests now ignore the discipline on celibacy, I was rebuked by some homosexual Catholics for seeming to assume that the forbidden liaisons involved heterosexuals only.) Whatever the ultimate church decisions may be, there are two points I would like to make.

First, the main biblical reference to homosexuality is found in Genesis 19, the story of Lot and the destruction of Sodom. Although it has traditionally been assumed that the "sin of Sodom" consisted in homosexual practices, many now believe it was not homosexuality that brought retribution, but the breaking of the code of hospitality. Jesus himself has nothing to say about homosexuality. On the other hand, he did lay down general principles that are binding on all human relationships, sexual or otherwise.

Unfortunately, we hear next to nothing from homosexual Christians as to what they think a Christian homosexual lifestyle should be. It's time we did. One thing is sure: other Christians are not about to accept less commitment, fidelity, or mutuality from homosexuals than they feel the gospel asks of the heterosexual majority. Nor should they.

Abortion

I

An MP friend called from Ottawa one day, asking me to explain my stand on abortion. "Although your position is the same as mine—anti-abortion and, at the same time, pro-choice—I'd like help in clarifying this for others," he said. His concern was that at first glance, such a view seems paradoxical. Certainly it would be much simpler to be able to brand one's position as either anti-abortion or pro-choice. But the issue itself is anything but simple.

First, no sensible, thinking person who is committed to the faith that we are responsible in our actions to more than ourselves can regard abortion as a good thing in itself. Looked at in the abstract, divorced from all other considerations, the termination of a pregnancy at any stage is an evil. The fetus in the early stages is not merely a clump of cells without any instrinsic moral value; even the microscopic blastocyst or the zygote is a human-life-in-process, and it is worthy of respect. Thus, use of abortion as a means of birth-control, an escape from reproductive responsibility, is self-indulgent and immoral. But there are other evils. One is the fact that the present law effectively removes any choice from thousands of Canadian women who happen to live in remote areas or in communities without a therapeutic abortion committee. Another is the bureaucratic red tape that means many are forced to put off their abortions to the point—after the third month—where the choice is a great deal worse than it needs to be.

Moreover, to recognize irresponsible abortion as an evil is a very far cry from the doctrinaire view that all abortions are wrong. And it has very little in common with the oft-repeated slander that abortion is murder. To jump from the idea that a fetus is a potential human being or a human-being-in-process to saying it is already a human being or a person is sloppy thinking. Potentialities are indeed important, but they emphatically do not have the same value as actualities. In our Western morality, people have an ultimate value. Fetuses have value but not an equal value with actual persons. Specifically, they do not have the ultimate value of the pregnant woman.

At this point it is worthwhile quoting W.A. Criswell, who happens to be, surprisingly, a conservative fundamentalist scholar. Emphasizing the relative value of the fetus as contrasted with the ultimate value of the woman, he writes: "I have always felt that it was only after a child was born and had life separate from its mother that it became an individual person. And it has always, therefore, seemed to me that what is best for the mother and the future should be allowed" (cited in *Abortion: The Moral Issues*, edited by Edward Batchelor, Jr., p. 186).

It is this kind of approach that underlies the total absence of prohibitions against abortion in the Old Testament. Such silence is impressive when you consider the extremely harsh prohibitions against abortion in all the surrounding cultures of that period. It is also the reason why in Jewish thought abortion is never called murder. When the Nazis decreed that all pregnant Jewish women in the death camps were to be destroyed, the rabbis agreed that abortion was the only moral route for them to take.

According to the Bible, what makes us persons is our God-like ability and responsibility to make hard choices, our capacity for relationships, and our powers of self-transcendance and self-awareness. This description is applicable to the pregnant woman in a way and in a depth that is simply not true of the fetus.

There must be good reasons for terminating a pregnancy. But it is part of the pregnant woman's freedom and responsibility as a person to make the ultimate decision herself. To compel a woman to bear a child against her will, or to force her to abide by what others define as adequate or inadequate reasons for an abortion, is a form of authoritarian violence. It is a denial of God's call to her to be a fully adult person taking responsibility for what is best for her own life and that of her family.

II

The door to a properly calm, mutually respectful dialogue between those who are in favor of choice on abortion and those who, for religious reasons, consider fetal life to be just as sacred as the mother's has opened at last. At one level the breakthrough has been very small—the door has opened just a crack. But what has happened, in the late summer of 1985, is full of possibilities for further attempts at understanding and for changing the angry, violent tone of the current national debate.

Six officials from the Pentecostal Church, lay people and clergy, invited Dr. Henry Morgentaler to meet with them. "We came to the conclusion it was important and right to meet the man himself privately, and in a non-judgmental way," a spokesman for the church group told me afterwards. "We wanted to share our views and convictions as fundamentalist, committed Christians."

The fundamentalists, including a physician, met Morgentaler at a large hotel in downtown Toronto. He came alone; they had dinner together, and then a long conversation in a space reserved by the religious leaders. Both sides stated their reasons for their diametrically opposed stands "in a quiet, calm way," and then proceeded to a full give-and-take discussion in the same manner. Morgentaler described the civilized exchange of views as marked by "a great deal of respect for each other."

Make no mistake: neither side has changed its mind about any of the key aspects of abortion. Morgentaler is not about to close his clinics or stop pressing for more free choice in the matter. His views are no secret—though very few of his critics have read the detailed examination of his stance in his book *Abortion and Contraception*. The Christians, however, could make the same complaint: people who have scarcely opened a Bible do sometimes knock religion and the Church.

In any case, it is important to point out that the particular church group represented by the six takes a position almost identical to that held for some time by the Roman Catholic Church (since the mid-nineteenth century and Pope Pius IX). In essence, it contends that from conception on there is a human soul present. The cleric I spoke with said: "We believe the soul comes into being—however marvelous this may seem—when the ovum is fertilized. So it has the highest degree of sanctity from that point on.'' He added that the churches involved believe the only justification for an abortion would be when there has to be a choice between the mother's life and that of the fetus. "But with modern medicine that happens so rarely as to be almost hypothetical," he said.

Morgentaler's reply to this argument is to cite research showing how nature (or God in the case of believers) terminates as many as 60 to 80 percent of the "products of conception" before the third month of a pregnancy. This, he contends, presents "a big theological difficulty" for the extreme anti-abortion faithful.

Morgentaler said the fundamentalists "deserve real credit" for their initiative. Their representative told me he regarded the occasion as "an enormous step" in that he and his fellows could witness to their beliefs and at the same time reach out and both meet and listen to their opponent. "It probably won't take the heat out of the issue at large, though," he said. In other words, there was no illusory sense of some impossible, instant resolution of the dilemma. Nobody was kidding anybody.

Yet I believe that this association of very conservative evangelicals has shown the kind of imagination and courage all faiths and "-isms" should exhibit whenever, as in the case of abortion, a bitter social impasse has been reached. I only wish their deep fear of what others might think—"that we may have compromised our beliefs"—wasn't keeping them from now going fully public about the meeting. Such an action could produce nothing but good.

To members of the other major Christian denominations and any other faiths who find themselves part of this often tense and explosive controversy (including Cardinal Emmett Carter, Archbishop of Toronto, who a few months earlier refused Morgentaler's request for a meeting on the grounds that the doctor was only seeking publicity), there are words from the Bible that seem to be relevant. At the end of the story of the Good Samaritan, Jesus tells his hearers: "Go, and do thou likewise."

III

The late Gordon Sinclair, broadcaster and controversialist extraordinary, once told me he was constantly surprised and puzzled by the abusive and hate-filled letters he received from alleged Christians whenever he ventured to criticize religion. He was feeling the cutting edge of what is known as the *odium theologicum*, the bitterness that historically has always attended religious differences. There is plenty of it around today, particularly in the case of the ongoing battle over abortion in Canada.

The most thoughtful on the anti-choice side of this debate say they are appalled by the "un-Christian" attitude and rhetoric of the extremists in their own camp. They are worried lest the abandonment of Christian charity and respect for those who honestly differ from themselves should lead directly from verbal violence to physical assaults or worse.

Much of the violence against abortion clinics in the United States—some twenty-five clinics have been bomb targets to date—has been defended there by fanatics who claimed they were doing God's will. My own mail from readers bears eloquent witness to the vindictive rage lurking in the hearts of some who claim to espouse the cause of Christ. Many other columnists and commentators who have argued for a pro-choice position as the most rational and moral alternative in an admittedly complex ethical dilemma experience a similar response.

This is a phenomenon that cries out for explanation and understanding. Rational criticism is understandable. Emotional arguments also make sense, since the topic raises deeply felt concerns. But abuse, name-calling, and threats—veiled or otherwise—make mockery of claims to be "pro" anybody's life.

Some of these people are what Eric Hoffer called "true believers." Certain that their particular brand of religion is the only valid, God-approved truth, they compensate for their own inner doubts, conflicts, or lack of self-esteem by the fiercely held conviction that they are God's elect few. The legendary fury of a woman scorned is a faint whimper compared to the roar of rage from the true believer when it is suggested his or her tunnel-vision of reality may not be the only right one.

The fact that Jesus said absolutely nothing about abortion and a very great deal about loving your neighbor—even your enemy—means little or nothing. Imposing their revealed truth on everybody else is what counts. When they feel their argument is less than sound, they revert to the tactic of the preacher who put a note in the margin of his sermon: "Argument weak here; shout like hell."

They write letters alleging that pro-choice supporters have lost their faith, when what they really are angry about is the fact that we don't profess theirs. To claim to support choice from a Christian perspective is construed by them as deeply threatening. One tap from the hammer of doubt and they fear that their whole edifice could come tumbling down.

Others in the extremist wing of the anti-choice movement are angry because they had no control over their own reproductive lives and deeply resent anyone else having it now; they had to put up with the stress and strains—or the destructive fears—of unwanted pregnancies and are enraged that others might not have to. Still others see the issue in terms of a further attack on the family and family life. In their alarm they refuse to consider the possibility that, agonizing as it might be, the choice to have an abortion could well be taken by a couple out of love and concern for the family already there. Those religious groups in our society that support choice are no less involved in the support and strengthening of family life than those that oppose abortion.

One can feel some measure of sympathy for another segment whose militancy is fuelled by disappointment over their own inability, for whatever reason, to have children of their own or to find a baby to adopt. But it is surely wrong to vent the anger one may feel about one's own life situation, fate, or problems on those whose lives present unique difficulties, which they in turn must face alone.

Forcing women to bear children against their will so that others can adopt them is an immoral answer to the tragedy of childlessness. As columnist Doris Anderson has pointed out, there are roughly 100,000 children in this country right now waiting for adoption. They need loving homes today. But they are forgotten in the rush to champion the rights of those as yet unborn—even, at this point, not yet conceived.

The repressed anger at the root of some personal attitudes, however, can also be seen in certain religious institutions, which have lost nearly all their former power and control over human lives and events. And since sexuality in all its aspects is the one area where people are still very vulnerable to guilt, fear, and hence domination by the hierarchies of whatever stripe, any move to loosen this grip is certain to bring down wrath—clothed, of course, in the appropriate theological formulas.

For example, in the case of the Roman Catholic Church it is evident that, while there are obviously other concerns as well, the main factor behind the opposition to liberalization in matters related to sexuality—contraceptives, abortion, women priests, compulsory celibacy for clergy—is the desire to retain control over the lives of the faithful. But the Catholic Church is not alone. Similar attitudes can be observed behind the scenes in all the other male-dominated denominations and faiths with rigid rules and attitudes regarding this intimate part of human existence: fundamentalist Islam, fundamentalist Protestantism, Orthodox Judaism, Mormonism, and the Jehovah's Witnesses.

Legalized Prostitution

Prostitution is now an open, running sore in every major Canadian city from Halifax to Vancouver. Thousands, we are told, ply their trade in the downtown core of Toronto—many of them youngsters barely in their teens. And for most their "calling" has little to do with preference. They have gone this hazardous, mind- and soul-killing route out of sheer necessity. Prostitution always rises when jobs and money are scarce.

Rather than tackle the complex social and economic reasons behind this phenomenon—for example, by seeking radical remedies for unemployment—and instead of looking at the psychological and other causes that motivate the ''johns'' or customers, many governments have opted for the simplistic "solution" of legalizing bordellos. The pressure to do the same here is mounting steadily. This is a sad and fundamental error. It not only papers over the real problems of society, it fails to deliver the benefits its advocates so stridently proclaim.

Fully legalized prostitution, we are urged to believe, would work marvels. It would all but eliminate rape, prevent the spread of venereal disease through regular medical examinations, provide the state with its due share of income tax; at the same time it would remove the prostitute from the power of her pimp and, where it is part of the action, from the grip of organized crime.

Some advocates take the case to ludicrous extremes. I remember years ago debating with the madame of a Nevada brothel, the "Cottontail Ranch." She attempted to argue (she lost the debate) that legalized bordellos would do much to improve the marriages of the nation! This is nonsense, but it is surprising how many otherwise intelligent people are taken in and convinced by it.

Another argument is that legalized red-light areas in a city affect the incidence of rape. But there is no proof. In fact the claim itself is based on a myth: i.e., that rape is an assault caused by sexual need. It is almost always a crime rooted in hatred and violence towards women; it springs more from bottled anger than from lust.

Similarly, it seems reasonable that weekly medical inspections of legalized houses of prostitution would ensure the prevention of sexually communicated diseases, but once again we are dealing with wishful thinking. Medical experts agree there are new strains of syphilis and gonorrhea (and phases of particular types) that are virtually impossible to detect without costly, lengthy testing. To say nothing of the AIDS epidemic. What's more, if the doctor's visit came, say, on a Monday and the woman became infected shortly afterwards, she could communicate the disease to any number of customers before her next examination.

As far as pimps and organized crime are concerned, there are no guarantees they would be put out of business. There would still be the competitive need to promote the house in the community and to carve out a particular "turf" or clientele. Legalized gambling has not done away with Mafia and other crime syndicates' interest in that specific human weakness.

In any case, do we really want a society in which the government itself, through legalizing and taxing prostitution, becomes the greatest pimp of all? Without judging or condemning the prostitute, it is important to do more than simply moralize when we state that prostitution is an evil. It is wrong not because it has to do with sex or lust; it is wrong because it degrades human beings, particularly women. It takes a human person and treats her as an object, something to be used and discarded, bought and sold.

There is no use replying that we might as well legalize it because "it's always been here and it always will." Robbery and murder have a very ancient lineage; so too has war. Few would argue in their favor on that account. The truth is that the kind of laws you pass and have as a country make known to both citizens and the world what kind of view you hold of what it means to be human and civilized.

If your laws call for the cutting off of various limbs for stealing a loaf of bread, or the death penalty for seemingly petty crimes, it says a lot about how human life is prized. If the law says women can be purchased like slaves, its real message is that women are just another consumer gadget in the marketplace.

Playing God

I have always liked the story of the Anglican vicar who spied one of his parishioners working in his garden one day. Looking over the fence at the splendid vegetables and flowers, the minister says piously; "Say, Fred, God has surely done wonders in your little plot, hasn't He?" Fred leans on his hoe and replies: "Aye, He has indeed, Vicar—with a little help from me. But you should have seen it earlier, when He had it all to Himself!" Beneath the levity lies a profound truth. As we see in the great sacred myth of the Garden of Eden in Genesis, God places man in the garden to "dress it and to keep it."

In other words, from the beginning there was to be a partnership between the human and the divine spheres. Humanity is given a duty of responsible stewardship *vis à vis* the created, natural order. It is not a matter of control over all other living forms or of destructive exploitation, but of respect-filled, caring co-operation.

This theme is picked up elsewhere in the Bible, and most notably in the New Testament where humans are called to be "co-workers" with God. The Greek word used is the one we get our word "synergy" from: a divine-human synergy or (literally) working together. The idea has extraordinary relevance today because of the complexity of the ethical decisions facing us as our knowledge and technology take us ever further into hitherto uncharted—some would even say, forbidden—waters.

Think, for example, of the Rev. Jerry Falwell's remark that in the new reproductive technologies such as "test-tube" fertilization, or in genetic manipulation to eliminate disease, the scientists "are delving into an area that is too sacred for human beings to be involved in." What Falwell was expressing is the widespread and fallacious assumption that if you can label something an attempt "to play God" it immediately becomes not merely suspect but taboo.

In fact, the current explosion of knowledge and of technical skills means that, like it or not, our species is being called upon to do precisely that: to be God's deputies or surrogates; to be "co-creators" of ever-new wonders and miracles to enhance human life. This development was foreseen by the theologian Dietrich Bonhoeffer some forty years ago. Writing from prison not long before his execution by the Nazis, he predicted that in the post-war world the churches would have to grapple with the fact that "man" has now "come of age." By this he meant that, through science and other modern developments, we have moved from being passive children to mature adults. We can now shape our world for good or ill in revolutionary ways. The future is ours to possess in an entirely new and radical way.

It is an infantile attempt to regress to the sanctuary of the nursery to say that we must not play God every time some fresh scientific breakthrough occurs. We already play God whenever scientists work to improve a strain of wheat or develop low-fat pork or beef. We play God with every instance of modern medical intervention. For example, when Pope John Paul was shot in St. Peter's Square in May 1981, he would surely have died had he not been rushed to Rome's top medical facility, the Gemmelli Hospital, for hours of surgery. Had nature been allowed to take its own course, the cardinals would very soon have had to hold another conclave to elect his successor.

Indeed, it is at this precise point that the Vatican's arguments against interfering with or breaking the "natural law"—say, in the teaching opposing contraception, artificial insemination, or *in vitro* babies—break down completely. If it's wrong to go against nature by using a condom, or the sperm of an anonymous donor, it's just as wrong to give blood transfusions to a wounded pope.

Obviously none of this means that just because something becomes technologically possible it therefore *must* be done. What it does mean is that each such development must be the subject of tough, serious, and ongoing debate. Assuming the responsibilities and risks of playing God means using great wisdom and restraint.

Baby M

There's an old newspaper adage that says editorial writers are like mercenaries who stay up in the hills until the battle is over and then come down to shoot the wounded. Certainly that seemed the case in the flurry of gum-gnashing on editorial pages over the "Baby M" affair. But it's hard to see what all the furor over surrogate motherhood is about.

Few things are more central to North American culture than the concept of voluntary contracts where payment is made for services rendered. If a woman, of her own volition, wants to bear a child for an infertile couple, through artificial insemination of the would-be father's sperm, receiving in return an appropriate, agreed-upon sum for her labors, it is those three persons' own business.

There is nothing intrinsically wrong or immoral in such an arrangement. As a matter of fact, this modern and growing phenomenon is vastly preferable to the Bible version of surrogate motherhood (a truth those religious authorities who get so uptight about all forms of modern reproductive advances might do well to ponder). The Bible account, the most ancient story of surrogate motherhood in recorded history, is found in Genesis 16:

"Now Sara, Abraham's wife, bare him no children; and she had a handmaid, an Egyptian slavegirl, whose name was Hagar. And Sara said to Abraham, Behold now, the Lord hath restrained me from bearing children; I beseech you go in unto my maid. It may be that I may obtain children by her. And Abraham did what his wife told him. And Sara . . . gave Hagar to her husband Abraham to be his wife. And he went in unto Hagar, and she conceived . . . . "

Notice that the entire transaction was based upon coercion. As a slave, Hagar had no choice. It was, from our modern point of view, a form of rape. (It is worth commenting in passing that the institution of slavery appears everywhere in both the Old and New Testaments and, while it is humanized and ameliorated in many ways, it is nowhere abrogated. Jesus never condemned it; neither did Paul. This does not mean slavery should be reinstituted. It shows rather that there are indeed ways in which modern values can be more moral at times than arbitrary aspects picked out of Holy Writ.)

The second point to remark upon is that Hagar becomes Abraham's "wife." In other words, his first wife, Sara, and he are both willing to accept polygamy in order to have offspring.

Third, and as a logical consequence, this surrogacy arrangement involves actual intercourse with the third party.

One might imagine this could make for problems in even the most faith-filled household. And, of course, as the story goes on, this is precisely what happens. Hagar becomes contemptuous of Sara, Sara becomes jealous of Hagar—and very soon the affair begins to sound a little like the saga of Jimmy and Tammy Bakker. The significant thing about this whole episode is that there isn't a single word of condemnation or regret expressed anywhere in the Bible about it. Abraham remains throughout Scripture the model of radical trust and the pioneer of faith. He is still revered as a Patriarch by three of the world's great monotheistic religions, Judaism, Christianity, and Islam. Yet I can't think of any church dignitary or any Bible-believing pastor today who would recommend that couples in their flocks adopt Abraham's solution to his wife's infertility problem.

It is nonsense to talk about surrogate motherhood as the "selling of babies." What is being paid for is the very real work of nine months' of pregnancy and all the risks and discomforts of giving birth. It is equally foolish to talk as though a surrogate birth were not the result of love. While all too many pregnancies today are the result of sheer accident, the offspring of a surrogate arrangement is loved and wanted well before he or she is even conceived.

The only problem with the Baby M affair lay in the immorality of the surrogate's changing her mind long after the initial agreement had been made. If legislators in Canada feel any need to become involved in this issue, they would do best to regulate all such transactions by enshrining in law the validity of surrogate contracts and perhaps set guidelines for the fees to be charged.

IV

SOCIAL COMMENTARY

Consumerism

One of the things I dislike most intensely is being classified, referred to, probed into, or appealed to as a "consumer." Yet it seems there is no escaping it. Everywhere you turn there are consumer reports, surveys, programs, and profiles. We have been told we are "the consumer" so often, so loudly, that we meekly accept it as a self-evident truth. It is only when you begin to reflect on this quite recent phenomenon in human history that your mind recoils.

For along with this new name for humans comes something very insidious and dangerous for all humankind. Practically without our thinking about it, an entirely new and voraciously powerful "religion" has virtually usurped the place of all other creeds in North America and throughout Western culture. And its high priests have their sights set on global conquest.

This all-embracing system, complete with its holy texts, its taboos, its sacred shrines, and its electronic evangelism, is called consumerism. Its prophets predict a coming paradise in which robots and computers will take over every form of work and leave earth's inhabitants twenty-four-hour leisure every day of the year for conspicuous and eternal consumption of an ever-more ingenious cornucopia of products.

While most traditional faiths wait a decent time before trying to indoctrinate their children, consumerism greedily makes even toddlers into devotees, swallowing them alive as soon as they can be propped up in front of a television set or grab a sophisticated toy. Its missionaries never cease their ruthless yet subtle crusade for converts. Its dogmas call for a radical, lifelong commitment. The rewards? Pleasure ever more and more refined—and the envy of those less enlightened or less graced by the sacrament of cash.

Consumerism cares nothing for the stewardship of the earth and its resources; pollution and waste are its constant acolytes; and those too poor or so misguided as not to worship at its altars are seen as either unfortunate, benighted infidels or heretics beyond redemption.

Here is the core of the problem. Every age of history and every philosophy or creed has had its own specific view of what human nature and being human are all about. One's understanding of the purpose and meaning of human existence was, and remains, crucial for all else in living. In a nobler time, say that of the ancient Greeks, it was axiomatic that the key question occupying the best minds was: What is the good life for humanity? Everything else seems to have a goal or purpose, they reasoned. What goal or end made human beings different from animals, birds, rocks, and trees? They found their answer in the delights of the mind. Our forebears diligently taught that the chief end of man was to know and serve God "and enjoy Him forever." Human life was thus shot through with an eternal significance and splendor.

Some thinkers today, however, would argue we differ from the higher primates because of our culture's preoccupation with sex. A human being is thus defined as *Homo eroticus*, a hominid whose main impulses and aims center on sexual activity. Others say the best definition is *Homo ludens*, a hominid who is unique because of an obsession with games, sports and other forms of playing.

There are other definitions too. But they matter little because the view of humans implied in consumerism now has superceded all the rest. All of us now belong to the species *Homo consumens*, like it or not. The old creed might as well have been revised to read: The chief end of man is to consume, consume.

What this new faith does is turn us all into dehumanized, faceless objects to be manipulated by market researchers. There is nothing wrong with providing products to meet legitimate needs, but much of the time we are merely titillated into perceiving artificial wants. And to keep the system going, we have had to become a throwaway society just when a conserving society alone makes sense.

I don't agree with the present pope about many things. But when he lashes Western consumerism as hard as he does Marxism, he is right. Each is as materialistic as the other. Man does not live by bread—read consumer goods—alone. Ultimately, he can only be defined as *Homo spiritualis*.

A Plan for Peace

Ronald Reagan, the former good guy of Hollywood fantasies, now plans to project his disastrous game of nuclear cowboys and Indians into space. Having relished the glory of dancing a foreign policy two-step with Reagan at the 1985 Quebec summit, our Prime Minister now shows every sign of wanting to be a partner in the so-called Star Wars research—a Danse Macabre, a dance of death.

There is no inducement—no matter how many jobs are promised—that can justify our sharing in such an insanely costly, risky scheme. Unless, that is, we are so blinded by this offer of a "mess of pottage" that we will do anything, even if it means selling the birthright of our children. Having lost our innocence, our calling to be a symbol of a hoped-for nuclear-weapon-free world, through the testing of the cruise missile, we now stand holding out our bowl like Oliver Twist to the Pentagon and saying, "Please sir, may we have some more?"

Every Canadian who cares about humanity and the future of our planet must say no to this seduction before it is too late. Now is the time to tell our leaders by letters, telegrams, and every other peaceful means that the great majority of us want no part in this abomination.

The reason? Because the untold billions, even trillions, of dollars to be spent will take food from the mouths of the hungry around the world, lay crushing burdens on those already oppressed by poverty and disease, and plunder further the fragile resources of our mother earth.

Worse still, if it were ever to succeed, if there ever were to be a laser-beam "security shield" giving total or even near-total protection against the nuclear missiles of the Soviets, the whole concept of mutual deterrence—"the balance of terror" on which the avoidance of nuclear war has been postulated— would lie in ruins. You do not have to be a military genius to see that if one side were to become impregnable through its ability to destroy any incoming enemy missiles, the other side would then lie completely vulnerable to a first strike.

Thus the insanity of the whole space-defense scenario would lead neither to an end of the arms race nor to global security. At best the Russians would be forced to exhaust their already shaky economy by a Star Wars project of their own. At worst they might be tempted to launch a first strike against the west before Reagan's dream comes close to reality. This is folly.

But it is even greater folly to resign ourselves to simply beating our breasts. Solutions to the dilemma of avoiding a nuclear conflagration will never be found unless ordinary people decide to shed their passivity and to become somehow involved. If we are to say no to those who want to risk our future and that of our children's children, we have to begin now to summon all our creativity and energy and bring it to bear upon this crisis.

Following are two proposals for ending the nuclear threat and any further arms escalation. One is mine, the other comes from Robert M. Rickover, an American economist living in Toronto.

My suggestion—and it is perfectly serious—is that there be an immediate exchange between the Russians and the Americans of what would amount to political hostages. The actual numbers involved need not be that great, say one or two hundred from either side. The key to the plan would be who the hostages were.

Thus the Americans would pick theirs from the sons and daughters, brothers and sisters, and other close relatives of the American president, his closest aides in government, the power brokers at the Pentagon, the leading figures in the Senate and Congress, and the heads of the multinationals with the greatest involvement in making and selling military hardware. They would be sent to live permanently in Moscow or any other key Soviet city of their choice. In turn, the Russians would send over the same number of the nearest and dearest of all the top leaders in the Politburo, the Soviet military, and the armaments industry. They would live in Washington or close to some major missile site.

There would be some inconvenience and disruption for those chosen as hostages. But since they would come from the ranks of those on either side who have been and always are the most vocal in their avowals of patriotism on the one hand and commitment to world peace on the other, they could presumably be persuaded that their small sacrifice was a tiny price to pay for such an achievement.

Neither side would be willing to chance provoking the other

into a nuclear strike; there would be every reason for accepting a bilateral nuclear freeze as the first step in eliminating nuclear weapons altogether. The agreement worked out could stipulate that once the last nuclear device had been destroyed or converted to innocent uses, the hostages could return home.

Rickover, who wrote to me after hearing my proposal on a phone-in show, calls his suggestion the "1-percent solution." He urges a massive program of tourism between the United States and the Soviet Union.

"For half its total spending on all armaments, the American government could send a quarter of its entire population to Russia every year for a free vacation. There would be just over two million Americans, about 1 percent of the country's population, in Russia at all times. Meanwhile, of course, the same number of Russians would be visiting the U.S. at the expense of their own government."

He admits the political will to finance such an enormous program would take some time to develop, but notes that the physical constraints are not really that great. Two million people travelling each way, say every two weeks, could be transported in three hundred round-trip jumbo flights a day. This presents nothing like the incredible effort and cost involved in the proposed "Star Wars" space-defense scheme of the U.S. and the inevitable Soviet response.

Hotel facilities, particularly in Russia, would be strained at first, but many visitors might prefer to stay with families or in the temporarily vacant homes of those coming the other way. As Rickover points out, the economic benefits for both sides would be substantial. The American tourist industry could create hundreds of thousands of new jobs. The U.S.S.R. could use some of its dollar earnings to help modernize its farming and industry. Both peoples would come to know each other, and dangerous stereotypes could be smashed.

Most important, everyone in the U.S. and the U.S.S.R. would have at all times at least some friends or relatives held hostage, as it were, in the other country. "While this would not eliminate conflicts between the two nations, it would certainly lessen the chance that anyone in either place would issue, or obey, a command to destroy the other," he argues.

Both these proposals may seem highly speculative, even unrealistic. All I can say is that conventional wisdom is getting us nowhere—or rather, is heading us for destruction. In the past the politicians and the generals have always led those who trusted in them to the slaughter. We can no longer afford to acquiesce.

Refuge

If bogus refugee claimants try to trick their way into the country, it is naturally everybody's concern. But God help us if that injustice blurs our vision of the plight of the true refugee and the deeper ethical issues at stake.

When the Church stops caring about refugees, it has stopped being the Church. When Jews cease to espouse the cause of refugees, they are no longer Jews. When a religion gives no thought for the persecuted, the homeless, the "losers" of any era, it has stopped being a religion and has become an idolatrous cult. At a time when so many voices are being raised against what the Bible calls "the stranger within our gates," these words should be engraved on the door of every house of worship in the land.

Anyone who tries to take seriously a call to live a spiritual life—one based upon eternal values—has to be appalled at the red-neck jeers now being directed at refugees and all those, including religious groups, who dare to champion them. People who should know better are tapping into latent racism and its sources, ignorance and fear, to justify their own vitriol. This is a betrayal both of our moral heritage and of those desperate fellow human beings with nowhere else to go who increasingly come to us for help.

Not everything that every inter-faith or inter-church group says about specific refugees is necessarily just and correct. But it must be listened to and weighed with the utmost care, because if religious leaders cannot be heard and trusted on this issue, then they might as well close up shop.

Contrary to what many outsiders to religion—and even many who consider themselves insiders—think, religion is not primarily about holy places, holy rites and vestments, holy days, or holy clerical castes. It is about people, about justice, about the healing of a torn, tortured, needy world. It is about the naked, the hungry, the downtrodden, the weak, the wandering homeless. It is the very opposite of the all-too-common false piety that prays, "God bless me and my wife; our son Jack and his wife; us four and no more, Amen." It is the utter contradiction of the pseudo-faith that allegedly concerns itself with the soul while letting the body go to hell.

People forget that the entire Judeo-Christian tradition began with a refugee people, enslaved and persecuted, then running for their lives, then wandering homeless for forty years in the desert before entering a promised homeland. Futhermore, it is one of the most powerful recurring themes of the Hebrew Bible that God is to be thought of as a refuge—a "place" of escape, of renewed strength, of salvation. Caring for the refugee, the stranger, is set forth as more pleasing to God than any amount of worship or elaborate sacrifice.

Because the religious groups don't want to sound preachy, they have avoided quoting scripture in their current appeals on behalf of refugees. But if we aren't reminded of the real imperatives behind their appeals, it is that much easier to be sucked into half-heeding those who dismiss them as simply naive. Listen, then, to the prophet Amos as he boldly states God's view of things: "I hate, I despise your religious feast days, and there is no point in your solemn assemblies; I will not accept your burnt offerings. . . . But let justice flow down like flood waters, and right-relatedness between peoples like a mighty stream!"

Christians must never forget that they profess to follow one who was, as a child, a refugee in the land of Egypt, having fled the sword of Herod. They cannot ignore the fact that Jesus remains one with all the millions of the homeless and dispossessed in the world today because he never owned a home, never had a place to lay his head.

You hear a lot of talk in religion about creeds or dogmas. But in that solemn passage in Matthew's Gospel where Jesus talks about final judgment, there is no mention of any of that. The sole criterion for acceptance is not what one believed but what one *did* for the unfortunate.

"For I was hungry, and you gave me food to eat; I was thirsty, and you gave me a drink; I was a stranger and you allowed me in . . . ." (Matt. 25:31 - end)

Divorce

Alfred North Whitehead, the eminent scientist-mathematician, once wrote: "There are no whole truths; all truths are half-truths. It is trying to treat them as whole truths that plays the devil." (*Dialogues of Alfred North Whitehead*, prologue). There are any number of present controversies where this urge to push half-truths as though they were whole is "playing the devil." Take the matter of divorce. Few subjects occasion more misleading and hasty judgments, more exaggerated half-truths.

This tendency was glaring in the media reaction to Justice Minister John Crosbie's proposal for a national registry of divorce-payment defaulters. Obviously parents have a duty to support their children, and some system is needed to help enforce orders against the roughly 80 percent of defaulters who can afford to pay.

But it is decidedly *not* true that all defaulters—and let's face it, we're talking about men—are mean, uncaring, self-indulgent fathers. Many of them have been treated quite unjustly by the courts. Read some reports of family-law cases and you soon see how biased against men many judges can be—no matter what the law says about equal responsibilities of both spouses to be independent.

Many defaulters find their ex-wives not fulfilling their side of the court order: they have made it difficult or impossible to have access to the children. Some flagrantly use child support for anything but the kids. We need to hear much more from Crosbie about redressing this inequity than we have to date.

Then there are those who shake their head over the high incidence of marriage breakdown and solemnly tell anyone within earshot that everything is going to hell in a handcart. True, there are more separations and formal divorces now than fifty years ago. But there were proportionately just as many marriages then that amounted to "lived" divorce. The current situation is simply more honest.

Most of us have known marriages that were running battles, sheer misery for all. I remember one couple, leaders in their church, who hadn't spoken to one another in more than ten years, yet wouldn't dream of divorce. Even at meals they addressed each other only through the children: "Freddy, have your father pass the potatoes." No matter how virtuous it looked to outsiders, they had a *de facto* divorce. The "until death do us part" bit was history already.

Clergy and other moralists, who ought to know better, often say that divorce is "the easy way out," a sign of selfishness and hedonism. Certainly it is easier to live alone or with someone else than to endure a situation where one or the other or both are slowly going crazy. But anyone who supposes that the process of separation and divorce is taking some "easy way" has to be ignorant of the facts of life. For those who have felt forced to take this route there will be few, if any, decisions they will face thereafter that require more courage, or more emotional and physical stamina.

Religion, which purports to major in forgiveness, compassion, and understanding, too often acts as a condemning, guilt-reinforcing element in the emotional mix during a divorce. And no matter how reasonable the parties may wish to be, once the lawyers become involved the estranged couple are often driven to open warfare.

It is true that the family is under great pressure today; but a high divorce rate does not mean it is a dying institution. In fact, the urge to strengthen and nurture familial ties and to form new family communities is strong in the majority of divorcing spouses. Most remarry and, whether they do or not, they often try to make more of the time they spend with their children than they did before.

Again, it is obvious that marriage breakups affect children deeply, but this needs to be considered objectively if we are to avoid serious misunderstanding. Children are much more likely to be permanently hurt by living in an atmosphere of constant tension and ugly fights, which leave their parents with little love left to give them, than by a divorce.

Recent studies both in the Canada and the U.S. suggest that the vast majority of youngsters settle down to a very normal ethos of feeling and acting once the air has been cleared and their parents begin life anew. It is the process of separation and divorce they find stressful, not the final act. After all, they lived in the middle of the mess; they understand better than most what made the breakup the lesser of two evils. What really damages children in such situations is the cruel and selfish use of them by either spouse as a means of hurting the other. This is a much worse denial of love than any divorce itself.

Family Ties

Bertrand Russell once pointed out that there is no bishop anywhere who would dare to preach what Jesus taught about the family. This is worth thinking about. To hear most clergy and evangelists going on about either the nuclear or the extended family, you would think Jesus regarded their value as absolute, akin to that of God. According to the Gospels, however, he held no such comfortable view. As with many other things he is reported to have said, the Church has conveniently ignored his words on family relationships or changed them around to suit its own needs and traditions.

Christ's attitude to family ties was radical: they are never to take the place of one's loyalty and devotion to the ultimate source of all being, the One he called Father. Anything or anybody that takes the place of God is an idol; nobody can serve two masters.

Consider: the churches with the greatest claims to catholicity (i.e., universality) have always treated the Mother of Jesus with a reverence that has come at times very close to worship. But he himself had a very different attitude. On several occasions his tone is barely civil; for example, Mark tells us that once, when he was surrounded by a crowd, his mother and his brothers came and had word passed up to the front that they wanted to speak with him. When he was told about this family delegation, he looked around at the throng and said: "These are my mother and my brothers! For whoever does the will of God, the same is my brother, and my sister, and my mother." Clearly he wanted to create a new definition of family, one based not upon the old ties of blood, but upon the much wider kinship of all those who seek the new humanity.

Another time, John's Gospel says, when Jesus' mother wanted him to intervene in an embarrassing situation where the host at a wedding had run out of wine, Jesus spoke to her quite sharply: "Woman, what have I to do with you?" (John 2:4); a better translation might be "Woman, what has this got to do with

you and me?" While obviously Jesus upholds the command-
ment to honor one's parents, it is manifest that, as with all other
aspects of morality, he was concerned to understand this at a
deeper level. Truly honoring one's parents can never involve
choosing their will for one's life over the will of the Heavenly
Father. No prompting or coercion by natural parents is ever to
take the place of the duty to love one's true, inner self or to
obey the voice within. That is why, for example, when Jesus
talks about marriage and the fact that "for this cause shall a man
leave his father and mother and cleave to his wife," the emphasis is on the operative word "leave."

Most clergy and other counsellors are well acquainted with
the devastation wrought in marriages where one or other of the
partners has never truly cut the emotional umbilical cord linking
him or her to a particular parent. It is only too possible to be
of adult age, married or single, and to be dominated still by
parents—even when one or both may be dead. They are carried
within the adult child's own psyche. Jesus' command is to leave
—accept adult responsibility for yourself, your feelings, your
motives.

In all my years around organized religion, I have never once
heard or read an intelligent exposition of Matthew 10:35ff: "For
I am come to set a man at variance against his father, and the
daughter against her mother, and the daughter-in-law against
her mother-in-law . . . ." This passage can be explained in a
number of ways. What you can't make it do is fit cozily into
any of the usual clichés about family life.

Commenting on the verse that follows—"And a man's foes
shall be they of his own household. He that loveth father or
mother more than me is not worthy of me"—Russell says, "This
means the breaking up of the biological family tie for the sake
of creed—an attitude that had a great deal to do with the intolerance that came into the world with . . . Christianity."

We could debate that interpretation. But my reason for raising
this whole issue is to point out that there are real risks in trying
to solve family problems today by simplistic appeals to "traditional Bible values." Indeed, one of the worst family ills of our
time, wife-beating, has often been made worse and not better
by religious teachings that make an idol of the family and make
the woman feel only terrible guilt if she does what she often
desperately needs to do—get out and run for her life.

Animals and Medical Research

The shedding of blood in animal sacrifice is something we associate with crude attempts by primitive peoples to placate angry gods. But we ourselves are part of a culture that daily sacrifices millions of animals. Most of these are killed for food—something we seldom think about in the supermarket. Many become grist for the mills of fashion or other facets of our consumer society. Millions are used for research. Each of these categories raises significant ethical questions about our relationships with other living things, particularly the use and sacrifice of animals in laboratory experiments.

The fundamental moral question raised is this: by what right do we treat animals as legitimate means to our human ends? Who or what says our lives and well-being are of greater importance than theirs? "Obviously people matter more than dogs, cats, or monkeys," you may say.

But morally the issue is not that simple. It is nowhere self-evident in logic that humans are of more value. When you state that they are, you are asserting a tenet of faith or belief. Such a faith may be based on the philosophy of humanism, i.e., that humanity is the highest value and the good of humanity the norm by which all else is decided. Or it may be based on the Judeo-Christian faith that we are created in the image of God and have been given dominion over the earth and all its life forms. Too often, down through history, this tradition—especially some verses in Genesis—has been taken to mean that humans have the right to exploit nature in any way we want. The result has been ecological rape.

Yet the chief model in the Bible for our relationship to the planet and its creatures is one of stewardship. Adam, we are told in the great myth, was put in the garden "to dress it and to keep it." Our dominion is to be one of caring, loving concern. A good steward hands over to others what has been entrusted to him—hands it over in better shape than when he received it.

It is out of this two-fold context—belief in the ultimate value of human persons and belief that we are called to be responsible stewards of all the earth—that I formulate my own response to the unpleasant reality of animal experiments. On these grounds there is no justification for the use of animals in experiments having to do with war, weapons, or defense. Nor is the exploitation of animals justified in the production of ever-proliferating cosmetics and other unnecessary consumer items. This is not stewardship but collective irresponsibility.

Medical research, however, is different. Recently, at the University of Toronto, I watched as a surgical team removed the liver of a pig in preparation for a transplant into another pig. It is precisely because of this operation and others like it—conducted with all the sedation, hygiene, and consummate care of any human surgery—that persons dying of liver disease will soon be offered new hope.

In another room at the university's medical school I saw a doctor preparing a dog for surgery in an attempt to discover ways of making heart pacemakers more energy-efficient, in order to avoid frequent operations for replacements. The dog, an unclaimed stray, felt no more pain than anyone who has ever been sedated for a similar operation.

After spending several hours there I had no trouble in accepting the comment of Dr. George Connell, the university's president: "These animals are extremely well cared for. They're well housed and fed and most of them suffer no traumatic experience . . . in the course of experimentation."

It is because of such experimentation that millions now live longer, healthier lives than ever before. (Our average lifespan has lengthened twenty-five years since 1900, and animals have benefited by the increased knowledge as well.) Nearly every advance in medicine—from Banting and Best's discovery of insulin for diabetes, to organ transplants, medications to control epileptic seizures, artificial joints, cataract removal and artificial lens implants, and radiation therapy for cancer—has been due to animal research.

Wherever possible today's medical researchers avoid the use of live animals. Work with dead tissues, cultures, or computer models is infinitely easier and less costly. These people are not mad sadists, but dedicated scientists bent on the relief of human misery. And their work with animals is carefully monitored by several regulatory bodies.

For those diseases still unsolved—cancer, multiple sclerosis, heart disease, Alzheimer's disease, cystic fibrosis, and the rest—research involving animals offers the best and, in some cases, the only hope of a cure.

It is for this reason that the extreme wing of the animal rights movement, those who would ban even controlled medical experimentation with animals, present a serious danger. As Dr. John A. Krasney, professor of physiology at the State University of New York, Buffalo, has warned: "If the current antivivisection movement is allowed to continue unchallenged . . . the steady advance of medical science would cease. All hope of a cure for cancer would be lost . . . ."

To hold that it is morally right to use some animals, under certain conditions, in medical research is not to imply that animals have no rights; nor is it to bless cruelty in any form. In most ethical dilemmas there is no clear choice between good and evil. Instead, it is one between two evils, a lesser and a greater. In this case I believe it is a lesser evil to experiment with animals than to allow human beings to continue under the curse of chronic pain and disease.

Native People

"We cannot account with much pride the treatment of Indian people in this country," a B.C. Supreme Court justice said as he granted thirty-six Indian bands a delay in CN's plans to complete a $400-million railway project through the Rockies. While the judge did the right thing, his pronouncement has to be one of the biggest understatements of the decade. Coming as it does in the midst of constant media accounts of the violence fanned by apartheid in South Africa and the torrent of passionately anti-apartheid letters to editors across the land, it serves to remind us of certain grim realities here at home.

For we ourselves have been involved in a kind of apartheid towards our native peoples for centuries. And the oppression and hidden violence, in spite of progress in some areas, is still going on. The evidence is clear: the high infant mortality rate, the unemployment soaring as high as 50 to 60 percent in some native communities, the way racist stereotypes persist more insidiously against them than any other racial minority. The social cost of their experience of oppression has been enormous—alcoholism, depression, violence, and suicide.

No doubt part of the reason this injustice has persisted is that people in the urban centers of the south rarely have any occasion to see how the majority of our native people live. My own experience dates back some twenty-five years, but I have more recently travelled extensively across the north and, sadly, I have seen little to indicate that conditions have really changed.

I was sent north by my church to teach school when I was training for the priesthood, between spring breakup and fall— the period when all the families brought in their furs to the camp around the trading store. That was the only time all the children could be in one place. Most of their year was spent on scattered hunting grounds running up close to the limits of the treeline.

My intentions were good. So too were those of the missionary, the fur-store manager, and the various officials who flew in every now and then. But in fact, as I realized only later, we were all part of a paternalistic system that kept the Indians in total dependency and did little to respect their culture.

Nobody had warned me I would have no school (I used the clapboard church as a classroom, with boards on trestles for desks), no adequate supplies, and only two or three children out of about fifty, from six to sixteen, who knew more than a word or two of English. The only readers we had were part of the Dick and Jane series and, with their white kids in city settings, utterly irrelevant to the lives of those eager youngsters. Three hundred miles from either a town or railway, my pupils lived in one-room log cabins or canvas-covered tepees. They had never seen a paved road, let alone a car. Nature was their mentor and hunting was their life. I did the best I could each summer, but in the end they taught me more than I ever did them. There was no health care worthy of the name. A portable X-ray machine was flown in once a year to check for tuberculosis. But one time the plates were all mixed up; the wrong people were flown out to the distant hospital, only to be brought back two weeks later. The ones who really had a shadow on their lungs had to be left for rediscovery some other time.

The missionary pulled teeth in his living room with no anesthetic and did basic first-aid for his flock. When he was away visiting other Indian bands I filled in for him, in fear and trembling.

Fish were so plentiful that the store clerk and I could have filled a canoe with lake trout almost any evening. The Indians would net hundreds of pounds of fish and then keep it fresh by digging down to permafrost and covering the catch with moss for insulation.

If a small commercial plane came in and got a load, there was money for a few. But often, due to weather or other delays, the promised pickup never happened. The fish simply rotted. Beaver and other pelts were the chief source of livelihood, but shrinking wildlife populations and changing fashions meant dire poverty and, not infrequently in winter, near-starvation as well.

The final insult was that as descendants of Indians who had signed a treaty with the Crown, surrendering millions of acres, each member of the band was paid seven or eight dollars annually as "treaty money." In addition, the chief got a new suit of clothes.

I recognized the injustice and failed to protest loudly enough. I was young and inexperienced, and in those days good Anglicans were not supposed to rock the boat.

None of us can take much pride in how we have treated our native peoples. It is fine to wax indignant about racial inequalities abroad, but it is still too easy to stifle the heart-cry for justice here. We see the mote in the eyes of others but not the beam in our own.

Rev. Thomas Berry

I

T.S. Eliot ends his poem *The Hollow Men* with the now-familiar lines:

> *This is the way the world ends*
> *Not with a bang but a whimper.*

They rushed to my mind as I sat in the main lobby of the Royal York Hotel. Across from me, speaking in a voice so soft I had to strain to hear him, was a man many view as a major prophet of our time.

Fr. Thomas Berry, a Roman Catholic theologian, studies the history of cultures. His special interests are the environment

and the need for a mutation-like change in our human species—
"the most serious re-orientation of the human since the dawn
of history"—if we are to survive. A member of the Passionist
Order, he is founder and director of the Riverdale Center for
Religious Research, in the Bronx, New York.

He was talking about the end of the world—not from nuclear
war, but from the collapse of all bio-systems due to human
exploitation of the planet. "Even nuclear war has to be seen in
a proper context," he says. "A couple more generations of plundering and it won't make much difference whether there's a
war or not."

Berry's analysis of our present plight as a species is harrow-
ing. Both the churches and the scientific community are bankrupt, he believes, when it comes to the environmental crunch.
"We are afflicted with the pathology of consumerism; all our
various systems and structures support the raping of the planet
process. The different religious traditions are making little real
critique or complaint."

For example, although the Church condemns suicide, it allows
us to "commit geocide [killing the earth] or biocide [killing living
systems] by eliminating wetlands, wholesale cutting down of
forests, totally eliminating the habitats of varied species, and
ruining lakes or even oceans."

Whether you look at loss of topsoil—"it's disappearing faster
today than in the dirty thirties"—and clean water to drink, the
negative climatic effects of global air pollution, or toxic-waste
disposal, Berry is convinced we are well into the final stages of
the surrender of the planet to total devastation. He sums it up
in this aphorism: "In the twentieth century, the glory of the
human [our technological, urban culture] has become the desolation of the earth." We are the most pernicious, most dangerous species ever known because, freed by our technology
from the natural limits imposed on the others, we can override
basic biological laws; there is no limit to our capacity for
destruction.

Berry castigates the Church for over-emphasizing redemption
and thereby ruining the integrity of the message. "Belief in God
as a personal, creative principle became increasingly less important; there was too much preoccupation with the personality of
the Savior and the church community itself." As a result, the

traditional "story" the Church offers no longer works for humanity in the "larger cultural and cosmic perspectives."

Though a priest himself, he argues we need a new "meta-religious mutation" in which we would move to realize the sacred dimension of earth. We need to return to "the Book of Nature, which was there long before any of the scriptures of any religion were written." We need, that is, a new spirituality based on the goodness of this God-made natural order. And a new, self-limiting ethic.

Industry must become "toilet-trained" regarding its wastes. Scientists can no longer create products and techniques with no thought for ecological consequences. "All human institutions, professions, programs, and activities must be judged primarily according to the extent they either obstruct and ignore or foster a mutually enhancing human-earth relationship. That is how good and evil will be calculated in the coming years."

Yet Berry's outlook is not completely pessimistic. "The lost species won't come back—ever. There is no doubt that coming generations will live in a degraded world. But a lot can still be saved. A lot of the natural order can be sustained if we act soon." What gives him hope is the way human consciousness seems to be awakening in communities worldwide. As he notes, there are some twelve hundred groups today in the United States alone "oriented to healing the earth," and about two hundred and fifty new ones come into being every year.

II

During my years as a priest I baptized hundreds of infants and young children. It was one of the happiest in a whole range of clerical duties. But there was a problem. I never subscribed to the outrageous idea that babies who die unbaptized are "lost" or relegated to some limbo where they are denied the full blessing of being in the presence of God. Hence there were parts of the actual service that made me most uncomfortable. It seemed absurd to be gazing down at some cherubic newborn while making pronouncements about its "original sin" and its need for "regeneration" and salvation out of this wicked world.

Recent attempts by the churches to update their baptismal

services are commendable, but the overall concept abides that the child is somehow already sinful and in need of cleansing from worldly taint. The full extent of what this attitude says about our relationship to ourselves and to the cosmos into which we are born was brought home strikingly to me while reading some speeches by Rev. Thomas Berry, a cultural philosopher given to such controversial statements as "The Church should leave the Bible on a shelf for twenty years and study the primary revelation, the whole of creation, for a while."

He said he wanted to give his listeners something to think about when a new baby arrives. Since we want to introduce the child into the world in which it will live, to the sun that will give it light and to the wind and trees, he said, we might do well to ponder a ritual used by the Omaha Indians, and in varying forms by all native peoples:

> Ho the sun, moon, stars, all ye that move in the heavens; into your midst has come a new life. Consent ye, consent ye, make its path smooth, then shall it travel beyond the first hill. Ye hills, valleys, rivers, lakes, trees, grasses, all ye of the earth, ye birds great and small that fly in the air, ye animals great and small that dwell in the forest, ye insects that creep through the grasses and burrow in the ground, I bid you all, yes all to hear me: into your midst has come a new life. Consent ye, consent ye, make its path smooth that it shall travel beyond the four hills.

This entrancing notion—introducing a child to the universe, instead of heaping up guilt—is typical of Berry's thought. Because we stand at a unique crossroads, when earth for the first time is subject to our decision—not just in terms of nuclear explosions, but also in terms of industrial plundering—he contends that the major task before us is to "re-invent the human at the species level." That is, we have to discover ourselves as a species among species and interrelate with each other and other life forms in an entirely new way: "The future is calling us to the shaping of a world that will encompass the enhancement of every member of the life community."

Finding our own integral place in the universe, he says, means realizing that every life form "activates a certain dimension of that universe." Our role is defined thus: "The human is that being in whom the universe reflects and celebrates itself in consciousness and self-awareness."

For example, the geese out on the lake, as I write, keep landing and taking off as they get ready to head south. Their flash of wings and wild cries are beautiful in the November sunlight but, as far as we can tell, they do not know how beautiful they are. It is human consciousness that says "yes" to their beauty and celebrates it in words, or painting, or dance. Our role, says Berry, is to do that for the entire universe.

One reason we are currently shutting down the basic life systems of the planet is that we have wrongly understood our religion as commanding a dominating relationship of "man over nature." We've had too much emphasis on salvation and not enough on the goodness of creation itself.

For more of Berry's thoughts, see the book dedicated to him, *The Universe Is a Green Dragon*, by physicist Brian Swimme, and the works of Rev. Matthew Fox, especially *Whee! We, Wee, All the Way Home* and *Western Spirituality*.

Celibacy

There are four major reasons why the Roman Catholic Church should abandon its dogma of compulsory celibacy for priests. First, it's not working. In 1985 a news story told how an Iowa woman, Maggie Olson, who had been in love with a priest for four years, had started a support group for other women in a similar situation. Her ad, running in the weekly *National Catholic Reporter*, had been answered so far by about a hundred and fifty women and twenty or so priests.

The story merely served to underline the fact that while many, perhaps most, priests remain true to their vows, many do not. I know several priests who are in long-term intimate relationships with women. On one occasion, not long ago, a woman came to my office alleging that her priest friend had broken off their relationship upon being reported to his superiors. She had documentary evidence establishing beyond doubt that she had had two abortions and a miscarriage during the affair and that in each case the priest had signed hospital forms as the father. Faced with this evidence, his superior admitted the "misconduct" and said the cleric had been removed from his post for "therapeutic counselling." He was unavailable for interviews and has remained so.

Second, compulsory celibacy for priests is not a core Catholic doctrine anyway. It has a long history in the Western Church, but it does not go back before the fourth century and has never been the subject of an infallible dogma. There is no warranty for it in the New Testament, since the earliest apostles, including St. Peter himself, were married men. St. Paul, who preferred celibacy because he was certain the second coming of Christ was due any time and there was so much missionary work to be done, nevertheless tells us that other apostles took their wives along with them on their missions.

What is more, the author of what are called the Pastoral Epistles (1 and 2 Timothy) lays down specific rules that the *episcopoi* (bishops) are to have only one wife. It is for this reason that the ancient Eastern Orthodox Churches have always had married clergy, as have the Anglican, Lutheran, Presbyterian, United, and other Protestant churches. Moreover, certain Oriental churches in full communion with Rome—for example, the Ukrainian Catholic Church—have always had married priests.

In his very sympathetic book about the Roman Catholic Church today, *The Pope's Divisions*, veteran journalist Peter Nichols says that informed sources in the Philippines told him "perhaps a half of the priests have a lasting relationship with a woman and the communities they serve accept this without difficulty." He could have said the same about several other countries, including Holland, and there have been similar cases in Quebec.

Third, celibacy is hurting the ministry and mission of the Church. Many priests who have struggled to keep the integrity of their vows have paid the price of their loneliness and frustration through alcoholism or other addictions. Many others have left the Church altogether, especially in the years immediately following the Second Vatican Council (1962–65). While there has been a slight upturn in numbers of those coming forward for ordination or for religious orders in recent years, there are thousands of parishes and missions around the globe without regular pastors. And senior churchmen have complained that the quality of those coming forward to serve is not always what it once was.

What is less well known is that it is the rule of celibacy that has continued to deter aboriginal peoples both in our Canadian north and in Third World countries from offering themselves as priests: not to marry and have children runs totally counter to their culture. The result is too few priests and most of them white or non-native. The Church thus retains its "foreign" feel to the majority.

Fourth, married clergy would bring to the Church a vast store of training and dedication, as well as the kind of insight into human relationships that can only be gained by personal experience. Among the benefits would be a much more human, realistic approach to sexuality and the moral dimensions of marriage, including birth control. No corporation in the world, facing a similar catastrophic shortage of staff, would ignore such a valuable resource.

Celibacy belongs to the realm of the discipline of the Church. As such it can be changed just as easily as the rules about meatless Fridays or Latin as the sole language of the Mass. If priests were free to marry or to remain celibate, depending on their own sense of calling and their assessment of their own particular strengths or needs, there would be more young men seeking ordination and much less heartbreak for those already ordained. What is more, celibacy itself would come into its own. No longer a cruel obligation, it would then shine forth as the sacrifice, the sign, and the gift of God it was meant to be.

Sex and St. Paul

When it comes to sex, few serious discussions get very far without some mention of St. Paul. This is not to say that the fiery apostle is exactly popular. Indeed, many over the years have considered him an enemy. I have yet to meet a feminist who feels much fondness for him today. In general, then, he has had what can only be called a "bad press" in the media.

The most frequent criticism is that Paul held an extremely negative view of sex and marriage. After all, did he not prefer that "all men should be as I am"—i.e., celibate? And was it not Paul who came out with one of the most backhanded ways of commending marriage imaginable when he uttered the famous words, "It is better to marry than to burn"?

But Paul has been much misunderstood. In fact, one can state unconditionally that his meaning has at times been deliberately twisted to suit other agendas. For example, he is often quoted in support of the rule of celibacy for priests in the Roman Catholic Church. Yet nothing was further from Paul's mind than the establishment of a celibate male priesthood for all time.

As a former professor of New Testament, with a lifetime's knowledge of Paul's writings in their original Greek, I believe he had what can only be called a very positive, healthy, typically Jewish attitude to marriage and marital sex. You can't see the truth of this, however, unless you know something of the context and purpose of what he had to say about them. It is by quoting Paul out of context and by ignoring the background that journalists and others have been able to create a caricature of his real intent.

In the first place, it has to be kept in mind that when Paul wrote he was fully convinced that the end of the world was immediately at hand. He was expecting Christ to return and wind up history. Since the end-time was imminent—a time full of perils and calamities—it was preferable for all Christians to remain single. They would thus be free to win souls and they would not subject new offspring to the terrible events about to engulf all humanity.

But Paul was totally realistic. He did not want any of that phony spirituality which claims to be free from the natural desire for sex and family life and yet leaves the person constantly thinking about nothing else. To do this, he says, is to "burn." He knew that people who are forced to be celibate but have not been given the "gift" from God to remain so can easily be tempted or spend all their energy fighting themselves. The result is not liberty to serve others but a personal impasse and much pain. Some priests today find themselves in this predicament.

The other point to keep in mind is that in most of his letters—which were real letters, to real people with specific problems—Paul has to fight on several fronts. Two groups or tendencies in early Christianity particularly concerned him: both mistook Paul's emphasis on spiritual realities to mean that the body and its needs were of little or no importance. But from this they drew totally contradictory conclusions. One group taught that since the body was secondary it didn't really matter what you did with it. In any case, they argued, hadn't Paul said that in Christ there was perfect freedom? So they caroused and carried on—and needed to be sternly rebuked.

The other group held that the body was not only secondary but evil, the tomb of the spirit. Thus to be spiritual you had to deny and even torment the body. These people wanted to abstain from sex altogether. Where couples were already married, they advocated living together as "brother and sister."

Paul hits these Christians just as hard as he does the hedonists. He tells them: Look, I know some of you spouses are avoiding sexual intercourse as if this is a drag on living truly spiritual lives. But all you are doing is putting yourselves in great danger of temptation. It's fine, he tells them, to agree on a brief time of abstinence for fasting and prayer. But then the natural marriage relationship should be resumed (I Cor. 7).

Finally, a point seldom taught by clergy, Protestant or Catholic: St. Paul makes a clear distinction between matters where he has a saying or tradition of Jesus to rely on as his authority and where he is simply speaking himself. Certainly he had no idea that he was writing Holy Scripture. Like us today, he was trying to do the best he could—under the Holy Spirit's guidance.

The Pope and American Catholics

Pope John Paul II is setting the stage for what may prove to be a horrendous schism in his 600-million-member church. Ever since he was elected by the cardinals in October, 1978, his agenda has been clear: nothing less than the total conformity of every bishop, priest, and theologian to the ultra-conservative views of a Vatican clique presided over by himself.

While praising the concept of collegiality—the joint sharing by Pope, Curia, and local bishops in running the Church—he has in fact increasingly centralized power at the Vatican. A vast number of bishops, priests, and lay Catholics around the world have watched with mounting incredulity and anger—and sorrow—as he has castrated renewal in the Dutch Church, whipped the Jesuits into line, threatened the Franciscans, and hounded leading progressive theologians in Europe and Latin America. Two moves, however, are precipitating a dramatic showdown, because in them he has moved against a target hitherto thought to be inviolable: the American Catholics.

During his American tour in 1979 it was clear from every speech and gesture that he wanted desperately to discipline American Catholics—everything and everyone from nuns in civvies who wanted to be priests to parents of small families. "Have more children," he implored an amazed throng in the Washington Mall. But most Catholics, not to mention a sycophantic media corps, were so carried away by enthusiasm for his charisma and style that they scarcely heard a word of what he was really putting across. Those who did listen thought he was simply showing the flag. Nobody in "the land of the free" dreamed he meant any of it seriously.

Now, with deep shock in every Roman Catholic seminary and university in North America, the truth has been perceived. Dissent is to be silenced, snuffed out, denied. The Vatican's censure of Rev. Charles Curran at Catholic University, Washington, which included stripping him of the role and title of a Catholic theologian, has stirred a roar of rage from renewal-minded academics and laity.

But the furor is escalating all the more rapidly because of yet another unprecedented and heavy-handed move. Not content with his policy of deliberately replacing more liberal prelates, on retirement, with men he knows will toe the line, the Pope has stripped the Archbishop of Seattle, Raymond G. Hunthausen, of the bulk of his authority.

At a press conference, the Archbishop, who is viewed as overly progressive by Rome, said the Vatican has removed his authority in five major areas, including moral issues such as contraception, premarital sex, and homosexuality, the training of seminarians, and further instruction of priests. All these powers have been given to a hand-picked auxiliary bishop, Donald Wuerle.

The writing is now on the wall for the entire American episcopate: shape up or ship out. Only in this case the Pope may have bitten off more than he reckons. What has been up until now spoken of privately as "the hidden schism" is likely to break into open revolt. As one theologian here puts it: "The U.S. is not Poland; the Pope can't act like a Communist party chief and hope for consent. We in Canada and the U.S. who know what true freedom is can never go back to a church that is pre-Vatican II and that's that."

Those who think the comparison with Communist totalitarian tactics is unfair should listen to what Liberation Theologian Rev.

Leonardo Boff of Brazil has to say about the way the Curia has treated him. He is deeply embarrassed that Vatican moves to silence him reminded everyone in Latin America of the way the military dictators and juntas treat their enemies—anybody who dares speak out.

When he was a priest, then a bishop and archbishop in Poland, John Paul was very much in favor of dissent. Now, as he attempts to wipe it out amongst his flock, the story is very different. Unfortunately, it is one that could end tragically as the two sides of the schism—the church of the Pope and his admirers, and the church of the future—actually split apart.

Leisure

The most damaging thing that can happen to anyone in a position of leadership—apart from the tendency of power to corrupt whatever it touches—is the raging malady I call "adhocitis": an inflammation (hence the -*itis*) of the propensity to do everything *ad hoc*, i.e., piecemeal and as it comes along. No time is taken to think ahead, to plan, to take the long-range view. In short, it means a staggering from crisis to crisis. Others set the agenda. There is no time to assimilate the new, to be truly creative.

Politicians are notorious for this contagion. But it has been known to attack popes, archbishops of Canterbury, Protestant moderators, and clergy in general. In the business world the infection is so widespread, it is attaining the dimensions of a plague. It is one of the reasons why the urgent, profoundly moral questions—of unemployment and mounting job dissatisfaction, of the impact of the urge to increase profits on the earth's ability to sustain life, of the criminal arms race—have yet to be fully addressed, let alone solved.

The people who strive so hard to expand corporate profits (in no way wrong in itself) apparently have no time to ask themselves an ancient question: What shall it profit a corporation, conglomerate, or nation if it gain the whole world and so damage it in the process that it is no longer habitable? In other words, *ad-hoc*, bottom-line thinking has a tendency to become blind to the realities of a global bottom line defined in terms of environmental catastrophe or nuclear war.

Easy answers, of course, do not exist. But all of us—and particularly those in any kind of responsible position—need to take more time to stand back from whatever immediacies keep beating upon our doors in order to reflect on the larger context.

Near the end of his primacy, I interviewed Michael Ramsey, then Archbishop of Canterbury. I asked him what he thought was his greatest achievement in office. His eyes twinkled and those bushy eyebrows did a sort of gymnastic for a few moments. Then he replied, "I'd say my greatest achievement was to have learned the art of doing nothing."

Ramsey, who is still writing scholarly books in retirement, was not saying he was lazy. He meant he had tried to master the art of cultivating some leisure time. No doubt that is why, whenever he was called upon to write or speak, he always had something fresh to say. His remark illustrates a great truth about the human condition. Genius or creativity may be "1 percent inspiration and 99 percent perspiration" but it seems that inventive insights or forward leaps come most often when the mind has rest from its normal duties.

Archimedes, the Greek mathematician, was having a bath when suddenly he cried out, "Eureka!" ("I have found it"). The answer to a problem he had been pondering came unexpectedly, at a time when he was not consciously tackling it.

The Apostle Paul was walking along the road to Damascus when he had his mystical, life-changing experience of the resurrected Lord. He then immediately went off into the wilds of Arabia for three years of meditation before beginning his ministry.

St. Augustine's conversion to Christianity hinged on an experience he had while contemplating in a garden.

Sir Isaac Newton, who once described himself as "a boy playing on the seashore . . . whilst the great ocean of truth lay all undiscovered before me," is reputed to have discovered the law of gravity while musing in an orchard.

Most artists, poets, inventors, composers, and other creative people find the same thing. The moment of intuitive insight called inspiration comes most often when they least expect it. They have done the preliminary thinking and labor, but the reward comes as a gift—from the unconscious mind, and from the Source of all being. Historically, ideas and cultural inventiveness have always come with increased leisure.

Since, according to the experts, we are now living in the first true ''leisure society,'' one might expect an unparalleled upsurge of human creativity before which all our problems would retreat and vanish. Unfortunately, we cram this leisure time with even more *ad hocs* (TV, or whatever) than in our working lives. And the truly creative pause never comes at all.

A Religious Hall of Shame

I

Many intelligent people today dismiss religion on the grounds that it's made up of nothing but a collection of cheats, charlatans, and pious-sounding crooks. They are mistaken in their overall judgment, but I have plenty of sympathy with their view. There is some shocking evidence to support it.

The following three items were culled from a single issue of the newspaper in January, 1987. The first one detailed how healer-evangelist Oral Roberts put a gun to the head of every faithful fan of his "Expect a Miracle" TV show. Never shy about the content of the various chats he and God have had over the years—mostly about money and how to get more—Roberts says the deity ordered him last March to raise $8 million: "The Lord said, 'If you don't do it, I'm going to call you home in one year.'"

His audience, in about two hundred cities in the U.S. and Canada, is largely poor, elderly, female, and non-white. Already they're falling for this "cash or death" extortion. The pledges just keep rolling in—while he and his family live like kings. It is nothing new for TV evangelists to work their audiences over, extorting money through applied guilt: "Your unsaved loved ones could go to hell if you don't see that our work goes on." But Roberts' naked manipulation of the gullible is the lowest blow of all.

On the same page as this outrage there was the story of two Transcendental Meditation (TM) organizations ordered to pay $138,000 to a former instructor for failing in a promise to teach him to "fly" or levitate. TM, a technique in which one spends twenty minutes twice daily intoning a mantra—usually the name of a Hindu divinity—was introduced to the West in the

1960s by the "giggling guru," Maharishi Mahesh Yogi. Having monitored TM over the years, I have no problem with its various claims about the value of meditation for health or well-being—though is worth noting that researchers have been able to match the TM results by having people meditate using any sound as a "mantra".

In the late 1970s, however, the TM hype claimed that when a certain percentage of the population practises this type of meditation you get the "Maharishi Effect": weather improves, there are fewer road accidents, crime rates drop—and other similar nonsense. Then they began offering expensive courses in the "higher powers," including the ability to "think" oneself off the floor and into mid-air. Press kits included pictures of persons sitting in the lotus position apparently flying. It turned out that the pictures were taken by a high-speed camera when the meditators were bouncing. All requests to photograph or even be present at such sessions were turned down. It is shocking that the TM organization is still mixed up with this kind of scam, and encouraging that at least one person has had the courage to take them to the wall over it.

Finally, and the most obscene item of all, the front page of the newspaper carried a story with the headline "A Cake and a Prayer—Reagan sent Bible verse with emissaries on secret Iran mission, Senate report says." Even Reagan's stoutest supporters on the religious right should have been wincing. They applauded when he used his obvious, self-serving appeal to "old-time religion" to attack the Russians, to justify his social-service cuts and massive defense-budget increases, and his belligerence in Central America.

But now that he has been caught lying to the American people, when he has swapped arms for hostages while thundering against ever doing deals with terrorists, and his dirty war against the duly elected government of Nicaragua has been exposed in all its devious chicanery, the sending of a Bible to leaders in Iran is meeting with all the cynicism it deserves.

Such abuse of religion does not mean that religion per se is bogus or an illusory quest. Deplorable as it is, the abuse itself is a kind of negative witness to the truth. You can only cheat people with counterfeit money because there is such a thing as honest currency and solid coin out there. In the spiritual marketplace, just as in the ordinary one, the Latin tag holds true: *caveat emptor.* Let the buyer beware.

II

Watching the increasingly feverish antics of the TV preachers these days I find it hard to know whether to laugh or cry. Mind you, when it comes to smiles or tears they're a tough crew to match. They can turn on either at the flick of a cue card.

Ernest Angley, the faith healer who has won a sort of cult following among young people who don't accept his message, but wouldn't miss his self-caricature of a Hollywood-scale evangelist, is one of my favorites, too. I will never forget covering one of his healing crusades—they took up several offerings in the two-hour affair—and the response of one man who went forward to tell Ernest he was deaf in his right ear.

Angley roared at the ceiling: "Je-eesus he-eal!" and clapped a hand over each side of the man's head with a thump I could hear at the back of the vast auditorium.

"Oh my God," the man wailed into the microphone. "There goes my good ear!"

But there is a very unfunny side to Angley and a horde of other electronic pulpiteers as well. In fact, at that same crusade he asked all those in the 5,000-strong crowd who had cancer to come forward and be healed. About eighty people lined up before him and he went hooting and hollering down the row touching or even striking some on the foreheads as he exulted: "This is the cancer cure: Praise God!"

I know of persons who have received healing through non-medical means, so I do not intend to put down spiritual healing per se, but I interviewed several of those allegedly healed for follow-up. None proved out. I then placed a large appeal on the *Star*'s religion page asking to hear from anyone attending the said crusade who could co-operate both in establishing their previous diagnosis and in documenting any "cure." There was no response.

Now two letters have come to hand that force me to add yet another name to my unofficial "TV Preachers Hall of Shame." The flamboyant Peter Popoff, whose show is called "Miracle

Ministries," now joins the likes of Angley, Jimmy Swaggart, Kenneth Copeland and Oral Roberts in my "gallery."

Popoff's emotion-laden, apparently spectacular healings-about one miracle every two minutes—come chiefly from edited tapes of his healing crusades. The evangelist-healer mingles his pitch for funds with affirmations about his own "in" with God and the way disease is sent "by the devil." But the two letters in question, both of which came unsolicited to an acquaintance of mine, represent a new low in the snake-oil approach of many TV preachers to the problem of "bringing in the sheaves."

On the outside of the envelope of the first appeal, it says: "Brother R: Liz [Popoff's wife] and I were having a hamburger and the Lord showed me this blessing that is coming to you through my napkin . . . Praise God! Hallelujah!"

Folded inside was a large paper napkin (mass-produced) with a pair of hands outlined in blue. One has written on it in red ink: "This is Liz's right hand." The other, also in red, says: "And this is my right hand. I've been preaching for 20 years but this is the first time I've been led to do this. [Signed] Peter Popoff."

The rest of the surface is covered with messages. The gist is that you are to lie upon a couch, place the napkin so that the two hands on it cover your face and then "whisper through them up to God." The accompanying missive, printed on lined notepaper to look authentic, tells you to write on the napkin "where you are hurting, spiritually, physically or financially," and then to send it back together with seven dollars "as an act of faith."

Recipients are told all this could be "your key to a miracle" and warned that the letters are not to be taken lightly: "Keep this between you, Liz, and me. Some things are no one else's business."

The second epistle, which came soon after, says on the envelope: "Dear R. This is God. He wants to bless you." The gimmick used to try and extract money this time is a small oblong of shimmery gold ribbon clipped to the page. Popoff calls his letter "confidential . . . from my heart to you" and again commits the obscenity of saying the enclosed message comes directly to him from God. God promises, à la Popoff, to give financial blessings and health "even for that loved one upon your heart." All one has to do is get or borrow (!!) one hundred dollars, send it to Popoff together with half of the ribbon (he calls it a "golden mantle"), and place the other half in one's wallet.

The aim of all this, Popoff says, is to give the donor a three-fold miracle and to reach "over 10,000 souls for Christ." There is no mention of where these "souls" are or how they are to be won. The whole thing is little better than a sacrilegious scam. In fact, research shows clearly that TV evangelism is not "winning souls," since the overwhelming majority of its viewers are from the ranks of the converted.

My advice to my friend and to anyone who receives similarly sick appeals in the name of religion is to pop-them-off in the nearest trash can at once.

Religious Illiteracy

Various polls over the past decade, particularly those of Lethbridge sociologist Reginald Bibby, show that whereas at the close of World War II two out of three Canadian young people were receiving religious instruction, today the figure stands at less than one out of three. Just when religion is playing an increasing role in world affairs, we are raising a generation of, for the most part, religious illiterates. Yet students can't begin to understand the vast heritage of English literature unless they are familiar with the Bible. They can't comprehend the drama now playing in the Persian Gulf, with all its very real possibilities for igniting World War III, unless they grasp the religious background of the tensions there. Similarly, it is impossible to know what is going on in U.S. politics today without an awareness of the politics of the evangelical right and its religious roots.

Sunday schools, where they still exist, are largely an unfunny joke—church basements where well-meaning but ill-informed teenagers perpetuate the folly of the blind leading the blind. And where the teachers are older, it is too often a case of the bland leading the bland.

Two cases before the Supreme Court of Ontario in August, 1987, one in a Divisional Court, the other before the Court of Appeal, illustrate some of the more scandalous results of trying to inculcate sectarian dogmas in the multicultural, pluralistic setting of our present public schools. The first involves Andrea

Millington, the eleven-year-old daughter of Baha'i parents in St. Thomas, who four years ago began having nightmares that the devil was after her and that she was going to burn in hell.

In 1983, when she was in Grade 2, Andrea attended twice-weekly thirty-minute classes in religion taught by a fundamentalist lay preacher. The Canadian Civil Liberties Association has taken up the case on the Millingtons' behalf and has asked the courts to declare the religious curriculum of the Elgin County Schoolboard illegal. Their argument is that the course is sheer indoctrination in fundamentalist Christianity.

Obviously it is—and ought not to be allowed. Yet under current Ontario law, school boards are supposed to provide two half-hour periods in religious education—with no definition of what this instruction should entail. Most boards simply ignore the rule and do nothing.

The other case to be heard involves a challenge to the use of the Lord's Prayer in required opening exercises, and here again justice is on the side of the challengers. It is supremely ironic that anybody should be *made* to recite the Lord's Prayer (which should more properly be called the Disciples' Prayer, since Jesus gave it in answer to Peter's request, "Lord, teach us to pray")—forced prayer is a mockery close to blasphemy. As Jesus himself taught, any prayer that consists in endless repetitions is mere superstition and gobbledygook: "When you pray, do not go on using meaningless repetitive phrases as the Gentiles do. For they think their flood of words will gain them an answer" (Matt. 6:7).

Out of concern for this chaotic situation, and aware that many religious groups now feel a real sense of injustice and alienation in the wake of the Supreme Court ruling that full funding for Roman Catholic schools is constitutional, the Anglican bishops of central Canada have come up with a creative proposal. It has relevance for the entire Canadian educational scene.

Headed by the Archbishop of Ontario, Most Rev. John Bothwell, the bishops have issued a "Call for Action." Together with clergy of the other non-Roman Catholic denominations and faiths, they are asking for an inter-faith curriculum in Ontario elementary and secondary schools.

Noting that our fragile social fabric "will split" unless students are exposed to each other's beliefs and values, they want religious issues and values taught "objectively and sympathetically'' by fully trained experts. The beliefs of the various religions now making up our spiritual mosaic would be taught just like any other subject; aspects of religion would also be identified and thought about whenever they come up in other subjects—for example, in history or sex education.

Sacred literature should be looked at in terms of its religious, literary, and historical value, the bishops say. Students should be helped to reflect on what it means to be a religious person, what part the various faiths play in their communities, and how each faith meets the urgent question of the meaning of life. The bishops have asked Premier David Peterson's government to set up an inter-faith task force to explore their ideas.

For once the Anglican hierarchy is on the right track. Until their proposals are acted on, we will either continue to produce students who are religious nincompoops, or we will watch as every faith and -ism rushes to form its own school.

Courtesy

When many people speak of morality or ethics today they nearly always are referring to sex. But those who are sexually without blemish may still be far from moral, through neglect of other virtues. Lord Bertrand Russell once wisely wrote, in his *Why I Am Not a Christian*: "It would be well if men and women could remember in sexual relations, in marriage, and in divorce, to practise the ordinary virtues of tolerance, kindness, truthfulness and justice. Those who, by conventional standards, are sexually virtuous, too often consider themselves thereby absolved from behaving like decent human beings. Most moralists have been so obsessed by sex that they have laid too little emphasis on other more socially useful kinds of ethically commendable conduct."

One of the most tragic casualties of the habit of equating morality with sex is what used to be called "common courtesy." Alas, like common sense, courtesy is no longer all that common. We live in a society in which the moral value of being courteous—polite, kind, considerate—is increasingly dismissed as a sign of weakness or wimpishness while its opposites—rudeness, boorishness, me-firstness—are celebrated as marks of strength and personal liberation.

You can see the proof all around you every day—on the freeway during rush hour, in restaurants or shopping malls, even in our schools, where one might expect courtesy to be fostered as the primary ingredient in a fulfilling, "socially useful" lifestyle.

Let me illustrate. On Boxing Day my wife and I went downtown to see a movie. We happened to cross a side-street just as the traffic light—which we had not noticed—turned red. Catching sight of the signal when we were already well out on the road, we decided it was safer to continue across. This meant a delay of at most five seconds for a car waiting to move out. The driver, a young man, blared his horn in a long, ear-splitting blast; then, as he wheeled out into the main traffic, he rolled down his window and shouted: "Open your f—ing eyes you stupid f—er."

Less than twenty-four hours after Christmas, and his contorted face as he swore was the epitome of murderous hate. Admittedly, we were in the wrong. But to yell such gross obscenities into a street crowded with pedestrians, including women and children, and to do it from the safety of a moving car, seems to me to be an admission of both cowardice and a lack of self-control.

True, being behind the wheel of a car can turn even the most gentle of persons into a raving lunatic. But behaving like a yahoo whenever one receives a real or imagined slight is not macho, manly, or strong. It's a form of barbarity that, if unchecked and sufficiently widespread, could preface a return to the jungle. True strength and personal integrity belong to those who have enough force of character to control selfish and aggressive impulses. True gentleness flows not from weakness but from restrained strength.

What I am about to say now will offend ten of thousands, and so I beg leave to lead into it with a personal reference. I have been a hockey fan all my life; when at Oxford, in the fifties, I won my "Blue" for playing in the annual Oxford-Cambridge match. (Any Canadian who could stand erect on skates for at least ten minutes could make the team in those days.) Nevertheless, I have often felt it regrettable that hockey was our national game rather than cricket.

Cricket encourages courtesy and manly gentleness, with fair play. Hockey, especially as it has slowly degenerated in recent years—both in the National Hockey League and in all the rest

from Junior A to the neighborhood minors and peewee mat-
chups—holds up before our young people the doubtful values
of brutal aggressiveness and moronic crudity of language and
conduct. At the professional level it is so rare to see a game
cleanly and dextrously played that even the regular commentators note it with surprise in their voices. Sad to say, even the
Russians, who once played with a skill that made the game
seem like ballet on ice, have now sunk to North American
depths and can handle themselves with their fists and sneak
blows as well as any NHL bully.

Yet hockey is so fast and potentially so exciting, it is the one
game that needs no violence, no bringing in of the Goon Show,
to spice it up. As the game is played now, my advice to any
parent with a youngster dreaming of becoming a serious hockey
player would be to say no. That is, if you expect or hope that
this youngster will one day embody some of the key qualities
that go into making a truly civilized, rounded person.

Courtesy, then, is no trivial matter. St. Paul, in fact, includes
it as one of the essential marks of the greatest moral virtue of
all, namely love (I Cor. 13). We need it and we need it badly in
every aspect of our common life. Without it, social life first
becomes nasty and brutish; then it vanishes altogether. As
Hilaire Belloc once wrote:

> Of courtesy, it is much less
> Than courage of heart or holiness,
> Yet in my walks it seems to me
> That the Grace of God is in courtesy.

Fear and Prejudice

You don't have to possess a towering intellect or hold a doc-
torate in sociology to be aware that racial prejudice is alive and
flourishing in Canada. Scarcely had Ernst Zundel finished
spouting his lies about the Holocaust than the trial of James
Keegstra took center stage. At the same time, recent research
into hiring practices in Ontario has clearly documented that racism is insidiously at work at a very basic level in our social life.
Other examples abound.

So far, the main debate in the media has focused on whether

or not prosecuting the Zundels and Keegtras of this world really serves its purpose. It does give notice that there are limits to free speech and that we are not prepared to sit idle while blatant hatred of a particular group is propagated in our midst. Yet, alas, in the process the hatemongers get a public platform from which to trumpet forth their malicious rubbish.

There is another danger, however, and it is two-fold. The prosecution of racists and the reports from time to time of research proving there are racist forces at various points in society can lull us into thinking that the problem has been dealt with. Simultaneously, there is a strong tendency in every one of us to distance ourselves from this particular evil and injustice. We read the news stories with a smugly complacent feeling that somebody else is to blame. We tut-tut about what "they"—the hatemongers—are up to. We see no connection with us.

But the racism that makes headlines is only the fruit of an amazingly hardy perennial. Its roots lie deeply buried in the human psyche—in yours and mine as well as in the obvious racists'.

Readers old enough to have been around during the so-called Golden Age of Radio will remember gathering around the set to listen to *The Shadow*. The program always began with a sinister voice saying: "No one knows what evil lurks in the hearts of men; (pause) The Shadow knows!" Then followed a maniacal-sounding laugh.

The Shadow, who was a relentless foe of crime, was putting in popular form a truth expounded by the great psychoanalyst Carl Jung in his little book *The Undiscovered Self* and throughout his teaching: that each of us needs to learn to discover the evil in our own heart and minds. Jung did not harp about people being terrible sinners or steeped in original depravity of some kind. He argued that it is only by recognizing the darker side of one's unconscious mind or soul, only by bringing this evil up into the light of conscious self-knowledge, that one can resolve inner conflicts and find healing. This is as true of the roots of racism and prejudice as it is of the ultimate causes of war. The bottom line in either case, the darkness that leads to prejudice on the one hand and violent aggression on the other, is fear.

It is perfectly natural for people of every race, class, or religion to want to associate with those of their own kind. We see this in nature and it is a powerful instinct that humans cannot deny. We like the herd-warmth of those most like ourselves. No one race or grouping has a monopoly on this basic drive. However, fear gives it a demonic twist. What began as something morally neutral is easily warped by fear into distrust, dislike, and then hatred of those not like us—whether in color, language, creed, values, or political affiliation.

At what is frequently the unconscious level, we fear that a group that is not from our particular herd, flock, or tribe may in some way threaten our status, privileges, comforts, values, even our entire way of life. Because they remain unknown to us in any intimate way, their "otherness"—in looks, customs, beliefs—so kindles our anxieties as to obscure, if not obliterate, the essential way in which they are precisely the same as us: they are human beings too.

It is this same fear that makes us project the evil we will not face in ourselves onto the other person, group, or race. If we can't face the greed, ambition, lust, or pride within, we deal with it artificially by putting it on the backs of others.

In his book *Dark Eye in Africa* Laurens van der Post argues that white racism against blacks there springs from the Europeans' inability to deal with the emotional, instinctual side of their own nature, and hence their dread at seeing it flow freely in others. Similarly, it is often those who secretly fear they are not macho enough who are loudest in their aversion to homosexuals. We hate what we fear most. The racial stereotypes we use to rob others of their humanity, and thus make it easier for us to attribute any kind of perversity to them, are really self-descriptive.

I remember once, when we had some clergy from Uganda studying at my college, how one African, resplendent in his clerical collar, bluntly refused to help another by carrying his suitcase "because he's from a different tribe." But there is only one "tribe" of humans on this planet. If we don't see and appreciate this fact from religious or humanitarian grounds, a pragmatic selfishness should bring us to the same realization.

We want racial harmony in Canada and elsewhere; we know also there must be an end to war. Recognizing the part one's own fear and aggression play in fuelling both of these is the first step towards survival for us all.

Research and Risk

I once marched down the High Street of Oxford dressed as a Canadian Indian—complete with headdress and war paint. In single file in front of me, in similar garb, trod several other Canadian students, including Thomas H.B. Symons, the future founder and head of Trent University, Peterborough, and Ronald L. Watts, future political economist and principal of Queen's University, Kingston.

We had challenged some fellow-students at our college, Oriel, to an international boat race—Canada versus Scotland. The race itself ended in a fiasco; Symons had led us in a boarding attempt and we nearly sank both boats.

The thing I remember most, however, is that even though one of our party had kept the beat on a small drum as we passed the spires and towers of the town, both going and coming from the river, scarcely anyone on the crowded streets gave us more than a glance. England, particularly London and the university cities, is teeming with characters and eccentrics. It would have taken more than a few ham-actors from the colonies to have raised a ripple of notice.

I was thinking about this the other day while reading yet another story about the risks and the possibilities of genetic engineering, the scientific manipulation of the very stuff of life itself. Because of the intrinsic fascination of such research, and because of the moral questions they raise, I keep a file on such issues. On perusal, most of the columns and editorials in it appear to be unduly negative—a succession of jeremiads. It seems there is always some moralist or other wringing his intellectual hands and moaning about the need for ethical guidelines, while offering none himself. You know the refrain: "Science is going too far too fast in tampering with the basic life processes; God never intended us to usurp creative power over our genetic code."

Of course there's a need for people to sound warnings about scientific research. Just because something can be done doesn't necessarily mean it *should* be. For example, nobody who cares about the future wants to see the creation of beings who are robots or clones. Nobody wants to see blandness as the dominant trait of coming generations. It is the so-called characters, eccentrics, oddballs—whatever label it is we use to describe, or to put down, those "not like us"—who give life its real color and texture. It is this flair for individuality that lies at the heart of what we mean by humanity itself.

However, an overly negative perception of the dangers — indeed, a false focusing on them—can dry up public funding for research just when we should be going ahead at top speed. There is too much potential benefit at stake, too much future healing and relief of suffering, to tolerate delay while philosophers, theologians, and/or government committees sit and ponder what the rules are to be.

It's not really a case of either/or. Let the thinkers do their reflecting, but meanwhile let the scientists get on with the job. It's not as though they were devoid of ethical principles themselves or incapable of knowing what key rights and values are at issue. We need to find ways to eradicate a host of human plagues, especially those hereditary diseases foisted on the innocent at birth. And we need to do so now.

Similarly, Canada should not be lagging behind Australia or other countries in programs of *in vitro* fertilization, embryo implants, and other new techniques aimed at the growing problem of infertility. There is real pain for thousands of couples in bearing this particular cross and doctors need financial and moral encouragement in trying to alleviate it. Too often they get the very opposite. Sadly, as in the past, the opposition frequently comes in the name of religion.

Sure there are risks and dangers attending all present biomedical research, and there will be others in the future, too bizarre to even be imagined now. But what advance of human knowledge and technology has ever been free of these?

What is truly important is to view this whole endeavor from what can only be called a theological or spiritual perspective. As modern humans, or "man come of age," we are being called by God to be no longer passively dependent children but co-creators with the author and source of all things. It's an awesome, but at the same time exhilarating, challenge and responsibility.

Pit-Bull Terriers

It was a summer afternoon, and I was walking around the end of the lake where we live. Some kiddies were playing in the water while their parents sunned themselves and, up in a small park, people were having picnics under the pines. With my dog Morgan at my heels, I was lost in some train of thought, totally at peace.

Suddenly pandemonium exploded. Without a sound of warning, and utterly unprovoked, a brown, torpedo-like streak flashed across the road and hit Morgan full in the throat. The force of the attack took my dog at least ten feet across the road, where he landed on his back, screaming in terror. A pit-bull terrier had a deathlock hold on him and was slowly but surely squeezing and shaking as he tried to rip out his windpipe.

I stood transfixed for a moment. Then, realizing Morgan's cries were already the gasps of suffocation, I knew I had to do something to get that ferocious brute off. I roared at the dog to stop—wasted breath. Having no other recourse, I kicked it in the ribs as hard as I could.

Though I am six foot four and over two hundred pounds, the pit-bull didn't even grunt. Growing both desperate and angry, I kicked at it several times more, but it was built like a tank and impervious to any distraction. Its single aim was killing Morgan. By now, his coat was covered with blood and saliva and I was certain his throat had been crushed.

All at once I heard an angry shout at my back and a burly Rambo-lookalike (long hair, muscled frame, stripped to the waist), the owner of the pit-bull, came rushing up, yelling: "Don't you dare kick that dog again!" At this point I was furious enough to tackle anyone, and he seemed to realize it as I threatened to give my attentions to him rather than his animal if he didn't get it off Morgan immediately.

The problem was, he couldn't do a thing with his dog. Its jaws had locked like a steel bear-trap, and no threats or commands made any difference.

Then, again without warning, it let go and tried for a better hold. This time it managed only to get the collar as I pulled Morgan back with a jerk. Still with the nylon band in its teeth it swung Morgan around like a toy—across the road again and then down to the sandy beach where people fled in all directions.

By the time the owner and I caught up, the pit-bull had grabbed again. This time he had the whole of Morgan's ear in his mouth; blood was spurting out as the cartilage began to tear in ribbons. We grabbed the collars of both and the owner tried to pry his dog's jaws apart with a thick stick. The pit-bull's eyes simply glazed over as he kept shaking and pulling to tear the ear off.

Finally, dripping with sweat, we got the monster to slacken for a moment and I pulled Morgan back out of danger. As if he had just been hit by a car, his adrenalin took over, and he ran crazily for home and collapsed. I waited only to phone the police (of course, when they finally arrived, "Rambo" and his dog had disappeared) and then rushed Morgan to the animal clinic. The initial prognosis was very bad—deep shock, possibly a crushed voice box, and other throat injuries that could lead to death. I am happy to say he has survived and, apart from numerous scars and stitches, seems to be gradually recovering his old élan.

Nevertheless, it was a horrendous experience. That pit-bull was a murderous fighting machine that could have killed or maimed anyone in that park. A child's throat would never have withstood the mauling that Morgan endured. And the master of the dog had absolutely no control over his so-called pet.

Since this experience, I have read that nine people have now been killed by pit-bulls in the United States. Three people in a town near us have been attacked and ripped open. How much longer will this insanity be allowed to go on? Pit-bulls should be banned completely and the would-be macho types who own them should have their heads examined—they, not the dogs, are the ones to blame.

Black and the Bishops

With Sikh extremists massacring Hindus in the Punjab, mass drownings in Zaire, and the continuing insanity of the Gulf War, there isn't much to laugh at in the news these days. But I had to smile at a recent headline: "Conrad Black Attacks Bishops for Trendy Stand on Social Issues."

Black and others like him love it when the churches speak out against obvious individual sins such as stealing, drunkenness, and sloth. However, when what is being preached hits them in the corporate pocket, when it challenges the ethics of what goes on in the marketplace, they invariably scream bloody murder.

The story in question was prompted by a scathing article in the Jesuit magazine *Compass*, in which the chairman of the enormously powerful and wealthy Argus Corporation explained his passionate belief that Canada's Roman Catholic bishops should leave economic matters to those who really understand them.

He accused the bishops of grandstanding in a desperate bid to get attention in their various outspoken critiques of the Canadian economy. He also castigated the Catholic hierarchy for their stand against nuclear arms, American intervention in Central America, particularly in Nicaragua, and Canada's defense policies. But he was harshest and most strident over the bishops' statements on the injustices of western capitalism.

Black is anything but a disinterested party, and he waxed eloquent, even vituperative, on this theme. According to him, the bishops are engaging in "reckless guilt-mongering," encouraging "the great liberal death-wish," and opting for no less than "economic suicide."

Anyone who has read what the bishops have had to say—most notably in their New Year's statement on the economy in 1983 ("Ethical Reflections")—knows that their paramount concern has been the tragedy and injustice of unemployment. They have agonized over the thousands of young people here who may never have jobs and about the mass misery caused to ordinary people when they are thrown out of work by decisions based on profits alone.

Black charges that the implementation of their plans would produce a flight of capital and skilled labor, a collapse of our standard of living, and a "self-inflicted, mortal wound to our industrial capacity."

He becomes so frenzied in his alarm over the way the sacred cow of laissez-faire capitalism has been given the episcopal boot that he actually appears to equate our present version of capitalism with "the natural order established by God"! This, of course, borders on blasphemy.

God is not the Ultimate Capitalist, whatever Mr. Black may think. Nor is He a socialist. In fact, if there is one truth that soars above all others in the Hebrew and Christian Bibles, it is that the Supreme Being stands in judgment on the injustices and futilities encapsulated in every political and economic system.

How people like Black can think that the bishops, or any other would-be spiritual leaders, could possibly claim to serve God and yet ignore the Bible's repeated calls for social justice—by Jesus and the prophets before him—is a mystery.

If nuclear war, American duplicity and terrorism in Nicaragua, and the evils of unemployment are not moral questions on which the Church can and must speak out, what is morality all about? Granted, not everything the bishops say about the specifics of economic reform must be taken as gospel truth—as they themselves have been quick to admit. But the basic principles of justice they have outlined cannot be denied.

If the Roman Catholic bishops—and the leaders of other major religious groupings as well—are to be criticized, it is not because they have said too much about social issues; on many of these they have rightly become the conscience of the nation. Where they are failing catastrophically is in their task of meeting the spiritual needs of Canadians at this unique moment in human history.

When questioned about the relentless decline in the ranks of those attending church and synagogue, it has become customary for religious leaders to reply that this is really a "good thing"—a sort of trimming away of fat or a refining of the committed few. The truth is that what they have to offer spiritually makes less and less sense to more and more people. Until they give as much vigor to this crisis as to social justice, they will continue to be increasingly irrelevant.

AIDS and the Communion Cup

Anyone who has been following the debate over AIDS in the church press is aware of a deep and widespread unease among churchgoers about certain traditional rites. Specifically, the furor is growing in Anglican and other circles where for hundreds of years it has been the custom to drink the wine of Holy Communion from a common cup.

The Anglican Bishops of Canada have sought expert advice and assured their flocks that there is no scientific evidence connecting any known case of AIDS with the common cup. Nevertheless, they have said that those who are concerned should feel free either to take the bread (usually a wafer) only or to dip it into the wine instead of drinking—a practice known as intinction.

But it is evident from letters to the editor that many of the faithful are abstaining from this central sacrament completely rather than run any risk. Some are calling for a switch from the common cup to tiny individual cups or glasses such as are used in the United Church and many other Protestant denominations. Given the catastrophic nature of the AIDS crisis and our current state of uncertainty about some key aspects of how the virus behaves, I think the practice of the common cup, as traditionally understood, should be abandoned entirely.

What I have to say at this point is not particularly nice, but it is part of the urgent reality that must be taken into account in dealing with this issue. Having once been an Anglican priest, I have given Holy Communion to thousands of people at countless services.

In giving Communion with the common cup, the priest passes along the row of communicants and allows each person to take a small sip. After each, he wipes the lip of the cup with a clean linen cloth, turns the cup slightly, and offers it to the next. Frequently there is lipstick on the rim; not infrequently there is saliva. Occasionally (how, it is hard to know) there is a trace of saliva and/or wafer crumbs left in the wine itself. The priest has to consume any wine remaining in the cup at the end of the service, and he often finds some sediment of bread or wafer floating in the bottom of the cup. Contrary to what a lot of parishioners suppose, there is no special disinfectant on the linen cloth used for wiping the cup. By the end of the service, the cloths used can be quite soiled.

Now, the common wisdom about AIDS currently is that it can only be spread by intimate sexual contact with a person infected by the AIDS virus, by using infected needles, or by transfusion with infected blood. As a medical officer of health wrote recently in the pages of the national Anglican paper, *The Churchman*: "The AIDS virus is very fragile and can only be spread by the passage of the virus, found in body secretions . . . into the blood stream of another." The doctor goes on to say he intends to continue using the common cup himself. When I contacted Dr.

Alistair Clayton, director-general of the Laboratory Centre for Disease Control in Ottawa, he gave a similar opinion. He said that although the AIDS virus has been found in saliva there is "absolutely no cause for concern" about catching it from the Communion cup.

Unfortunately, there is not enough evidence in yet to make such categorial statements, in my view. For example, Dr. James Slaff, medical investigator at the American National Institute of Health, refutes the idea that the AIDS virus is as fragile as many tend to think. Unlike most retroviruses, he says, it can survive outside the body for hours to days. He cites cases where the virus has survived for ten days at room temperature even when dried out in a petrie dish.

Dr. Richard Restak, a leading Washington neurologist whose research involves looking at AIDS as a brain-related disease, says: "At this point, live AIDS virus has been isolated from blood, semen, serum, saliva, urine and now tears. If the virus exists in these fluids, the better part of wisdom dictates we assume the possibility it can also be transmitted by these routes." His next words are of paramount importance: "This disease is only partially understood, is presently untreatable, and is invariably fatal. For these reasons alone, caution would seem to be in order when it comes to exposing the public . . . ."

There is no need for panic, but there is for extreme care. The use of intinction or individual cups at Communion seems a logical step for Anglicans and others to take.

V

COPING

Anger

I

The past few years have seen a tragic spate of killings of police officers, to which the public's reaction, naturally, has been one of horror. Unfortunately, that horror risks leading us to some inappropriate conclusions.

In a culture where instant, easy, push-button solutions are demanded on all sides, the knee-jerk reaction of the majority has been a simple call for revenge. But violence itself is an attempt to bypass the hard work of normal processes; it is a desperate bid to short-circuit complexity through brute force. To jump on the "hang-the-bastards" bandwagon or join a mindless rush towards totalitarian-type censorship is to fall prey to the identical instant-remedy syndrome.

I oppose capital punishment because it is not a proven deterrent and because it makes every member of a society a participant in this same crime. No murder is more planned, cold-blooded, or deliberate than a judicial execution. I am in favor of tighter censorship of violence on television or other entertainment media. Freedom of artistic expression is in no way threatened by banning the depiction of violence for violence's sake. However, neither of these approaches gets anywhere near the roots of the dilemma. The killing of police is part of an ugly spectrum of violence that includes wife-battering, rape, and increasing brutality against children. Something is radically wrong—something very complex, which calls out for immediate research and analysis.

One thing is certain. As individuals and as a society we have done a terrible job of dealing with a basic, instinctual human emotion: anger. It is significant that two of the killings of police officers involved teenagers who fell into uncontrolled rage when jilted by their sweethearts. According to the experts, anger is inevitably a prominent feature in the profile of any police killer. The same is true of most rapists and the entire gamut of violence-prone thugs, both criminal and domestic.

But it is not just the obvious social offenders who have this problem. It is one in which all of us share. In spite of excellent books on the subject—for example, *How to Live With and Without Anger*, by Dr. Albert Ellis, or *Anger: The Misunderstood Emotion*, by Carol Tavris—as well as dozens of magazine articles, we continue to perpetuate in ourselves and in our children two equally destructive ways of handling our anger and rage.

Many are prone to angry outbursts, tantrums, even blind rages in the face of any frustration or injury, whether real or imagined. Anyone in the vicinity, however dear, has to bear the verbal or physical violence that results. Too often, such behavior is dismissed with the specious excuse of "a short fuse."

Worse, in this self-indulgent age of Primal Scream Therapy and the school of "let all your feelings out; it's good for you," there are some who actually convince themselves their "brief madness" is therapeutic. It certainly is not good for the health of those who have to suffer it, and the experts now say it can lead to heart disease and other ailments in the rager himself. Giving in to such excess is to sow the seeds of violence to come.

Yet to deny that our anger exists, and to repress it for fear of losing the approval of others, is much more common and equally damaging. It can cause severe depression, high blood pressure, acute anxiety, spastic colon, and a host of other ailments. Sometimes it wells up out of control, and we are surprised that such a "quiet" person could be so savage.

We need to admit and face our anger as a part of our humanity essential for survival and in the quest for justice. We need to learn how and when to show it. Above all we need to know how to harness its enormous energy constructively in our lives, and to pass this wisdom on to the young.

II

You don't have to be a psychologist to find black humor in the violent tone often taken by those opposed to violence in society. There is a self-righteous hypocrisy here that reminds me of a bumper-sticker I once saw in Belfast: "If you say I'm violent, I'll kill you!"

There is much more violence locked in the gut of every one of us than we would care to have flashed on a screen for all to see. Which is another way of saying that we all, in varying degrees, have difficulty in dealing with our anger. We can harness the atom, transplant body organs, take trips in outer space, or gather the whole world around a single television event, yet we still know so little about ourselves. Technological mastery has not been balanced with self-mastery. The present nuclear crisis is the full measure of our failure.

Children learn how to use computers and play Star Wars games, but nobody teaches them how to deal creatively with their basic emotions. Adults go through retraining for jobs, but few get any help in fundamental life skills. Most simply muddle along wondering why "things" so seldom seem to go right.

Our churches, temples, and synagogues haven't been much help. The pews, and often the pulpits, are filled with people who have been indoctrinated with the view that it's not nice to be angry. Anger, they have been told, is one of the Seven Deadly Sins. The result is that extremely religious people tend to suffer more from depression and lean harder towards general intolerance than their fellows. That is the whole point of the parable of the prodigal son. The self-righteous elder brother couldn't accept his wayward sibling even though the person who had been really injured—the father—could.

Pop-psychology do-it-yourself books, with their call to assert oneself and "let it all hang out," haven't helped either. In fact, the two extremes—anger out of control and anger so repressed we dare not admit it even to ourselves—are equally destructive of health and happiness, both for us and for those around us.

Nothing can blight relationships, sow discord, and take the joy from the faces of children, spouses, or co-workers faster than the angry outbursts of those who "solve" their anger by taking it out on everybody else. What's more, this can mask itself in a thousand more respectable ways.

For example, we all know people whose entire life seems to focus on criticism—the worst kind is always defended by "It's for your own good"—or on snide, bitter remarks. Instead of looking inside for the problem, we project it onto others—perhaps "the media" or "the government." Somebody must be to blame for our frustration, failures, or general malaise; it couldn't be us.

Often, in the course of pastoral counselling, I used to meet with quite normal-looking, outwardly successful people who would say they were unhappy or depressed and wanted spiritual guidance. They would talk about any problem from sexual dysfunction to their deepest fears. However, the last thing they wanted to face was the possibility that they were radically angry with a parent, a spouse, a boss, even God.

The damage they were suffering—no energy, no joy, little hope—sprang from the enormous mental and emotional effort required to keep their anger from themselves. It's like trying to hold a beachball under water; it takes great strength and in the end proves impossible. Anger, like murder, will out.

The first thing we need to do is accept our anger fully. This means taking the time and effort to obey the Socratic dictum: Know thyself. Then we need to question whether our anger is appropriate. We may need to talk with a friend or counsellor if the issue is a serious one and we are unsure. It is one thing to face the reality that we are angry; it is another to examine whether the wrath is justified.

Suppose we feel it is. The next step is to deal with it constructively. Lashing out at the apparent cause seldom gets us anywhere. If a relationship is at stake, often the best way is simply to express the problem as coolly as possible. If we are rebuffed, we can then decide whether it's something we need to push further or can drop, having made our point.

Maybe we need to change our job, our relationship, or our own approach. Used properly, the energy released by anger can be co-opted to alter our situation or that of others. Creative anger has great potential for both individual and social reform.

There is a verse in Ephesians that throws a lot of light in this area: "Be angry, and sin not. Let not the sun go down upon your wrath" (4:26). The wisdom behind this verse goes back as far as the Greek philosopher Pythagoras. It means: Although anger is a natural part of human nature, don't allow yourself to be embittered or to brood over it; it will only destroy you and others; deal with it as promptly as you can and never allow it to become the pillow on which you sleep. That message is just as relevant today as it was in the sixth century B.C.

Fear

When a young reader wrote to ask what I thought was the greatest single problem facing mankind today, I had no hesitation in replying. It is not the bomb, communism, disease, or death. The answer is what it has always been, from the dawn of time: fear.

As Edmund Burke once said: "No passion so effectually robs the mind of all its powers of acting and reasoning as fear." Or, to quote a more recent figure, Franklin Delano Roosevelt: "The only thing we have to fear is fear itself."

The Oxford dictionary defines fear as "an unpleasant emotional state characterized by anticipation of pain or great distress—an agitated foreboding . . . of some real or specific peril." But very often the foreboding has to do not with a real peril, but with an inner torment of the imagination, the kind that makes one toss sleepless in the small hours of the morning. However figmentary this supposed terror may be, the pain is no less sharp or real. "A man who fears suffering is already suffering from what he fears," wrote the essayist Michel de Montaigne some four hundred years ago. This is as true of the fear of cancer as it is of the dread of dying or of the sudden loss of a loved one.

Fears, real or imaginary, lie behind the vast majority of physical, emotional, and mental ills that bedevil our society. And what is true of the microcosm of the individual or a particular community is true also of the international scene. The tensions and anxieties now being played out in the arena of world affairs, including the potentially lethal confrontation of the two major power blocs, are simply the projection on a global screen of the conflicts and terrors in the hearts and minds of ordinary people.

When nations speak about national security (and what evils are now done under this mask!), they are in reality talking about their fears. The entire nuclear scenario has its roots in fear. So too has the insanity of the armaments race, the increasing use of torture as a political tool, and the ongoing oppression of women in every walk of life, from the Church to the world of business. The results, of course, are catastrophic—misery for the individual and the greatest, most horrific insecurity internationally the human race has ever known.

But if fear is the only real, ultimate enemy of human happiness and well-being, wherein lies the remedy? How can you or I deal with this "stranger" whom we know more intimately than our closest friend? Philosophers have always offered knowledge as the clue. The Greeks said: "Know thyself"; Emerson argued: "Knowledge is the antidote to fear."

And there is some truth in this. As I have noted before, the reason December 25 was arbitrarily chosen by the Church as the birthday of Jesus was to replace various pagan festivals that took place at that time to celebrate the "rebirth" of the sun after the winter solstice. Behind the old festivals lay the real fear that as the sun reached the shortest day of the year it might die or disappear altogether. Obviously, scientific knowledge of the solar system has removed that primitive terror. By analogy, we can apply this same principle to most other areas of life. Knowledge of human sexuality, for example, has removed previously crippling fears from the minds of millions in our generation. The person suffering from irrational anxieties—say, a fear of crowds, of open places, of flying—can often be healed by being helped to know the original cause of the phobia.

Yet knowledge alone is often not enough. Sometimes, as in the parable, we toss out one fear only to leave a vacuum into which seven others immediately storm. Nuclear knowledge has only increased our fears a million-fold. It is at this point that we need to move to another level altogether. The effectual answer to fear lies, in the last analysis, in the spiritual realm. It is a matter of faith and of love.

Both these realities are debased and cheapened by unthinking overuse or sheer exploitation. But they remain the most powerful forces in the world to overcome fear, to "move mountains," and to triumph even over the grave. This is at bottom the message of all true religion.

When the trembling shepherds were filled with dread, the

voice of an angel said: "Fear not." Throughout the Bible the words "be not afraid" ring out like a clarion trumpet call. This is no idle bid to "buck up" or "keep a stiff upper lip"—it is not a matter of spiritual whistling in the dark. It is a summons to replace fear with faith and courage based on very specific promises of God.

You are always given a reason why fear is no longer appropriate. Isaiah 41:10 (a verse that should be repeated constantly by those overwhelmed by fears) sums it up best: "Fear thou not; for I am with thee: be not dismayed for I am thy God: I will strengthen thee; yes, I will uphold thee with . . . my hand."

The life and teaching of Jesus make no sense unless you hear echoing through it all his constant challenge to us to drop our fears, to lock on to a basic sense of trust. Contrary to what many think, he saw fear, not sin, as humanity's real foe; and his call to trust was not a matter of assenting to statements or creeds, but a child-like acceptance of the truth that behind and beneath and above and within every one of us a spiritual or heavenly presence dwells, a spirit of love more caring than any earthly parent can ever be. He will never let you go.

It is by responding in trust and love to this unseen yet universal spirit that the individual expels his or her fears and begins to experience peace. And it is only as the mass of individuals of every tribe and nation themselves know peace that peace on earth will ever come.

What Makes Life Worth Living?

There was a very wise professor at Balliol College, Oxford, while I was an undergraduate; I don't remember his name. I was a member of Oriel College, but went to his lectures because of reports they were not to be missed. He introduced the course by saying: "The single most fundamental question a person can ever ask himself is, 'Why should I not commit suicide?' To have answered this question is to have formulated one's own philosophy of life." Like Wilfred Sheed, who once said that "suicide is about life, being in fact the sincerest form of criticism life gets," the professor was in no way encouraging self-destruction. He was trying to compel his listeners to ask themselves some very profound questions about their basis for living; about what gives us ultimate hope, meaning, a reason for enduring mental, emotional, and physical hardship; about what it is that underpins our striving, our dreams for tomorrow and our joys of today. In short, upon what foundation is built our belief that, come what may, life is worth living?

Facing this issue is a highly individual, personal affair. And in a culture where you can buy technological gadgetry to do almost everything, it remains one thing you have to do for yourself, alone.

As anyone over thirty knows, the slick, superficial answers thrown up in our society on every side will always let you down. Personal appearance, popularity, success, sensual pleasures, material possessions, health—even our families and friends—all have their rightful place, but in and of themselves they are not enough. You can jog or dancercize yourself silly, eat tofu until you look like it—nothing can reverse the edict of mortality. We grow old, we grow weaker, and we die.

Repeatedly, recently, I find myself having conversations with those whom the world would judge to "have it made," and what they are basically saying is: "Is this all there is?" Or, as one of them put it: "If one of my children said to me, 'Daddy, are you happy?' I would not know what to say."

For myself—and I lay no claims to superior insight, or higher attainments of happiness than others—the answer to the professor's query is a spiritual one. I say "spiritual" rather than "religious" because religion so often gets identified with externals and trappings, to the point where the central reality to which it bears witness—God, the ground of all being, the cosmic mind—is obliterated.

I respect the courage of those professing to be atheists or agnostics, who claim to stand with their heads "bloody, but unbowed"; to be, with W.E. Henley, "the master of my fate . . . the captain of my soul"; who face life and the universe utterly devoid of belief in the eternal. But both my reason and my intuition tell me they are wrong. In any case, their solution to the problem would never work for me. Suffering, pain, and evil pose great difficulties for one who trusts in a living God in and about and above this cosmos. But without God they become totally meaningless, insurmountably tragic, darkness beyond hope of light.

So it is for all the other challenges and ecstasies of living. If ultimately all that we have striven for, and all those we have loved, are fated, with us, to go mutely to oblivion, then all of it seems hollow and illusory, a mindless cosmic joke.

I am writing this by the shore of a small lake whose dancing waters seem, in the spring sunlight, to be celebrating their release from their winter prison of ice. This morning I walked through a hardwood bush not far from home where the wall-to-wall trilliums are about to burst forth. There were turtles sunning and geese and ducks in a chain of ponds. Whitethroats and song sparrows filled the still-bare branches with their melody.

All of this is beautiful in its own right. But nature, too, is subject to transition and decay. Its beauty moves me most because it testifies to a source of loveliness far beyond itself; it is like a glimpse or foretaste of a glory yet to be revealed. It is the same with the intimate rapture of being in love, of listening to Mozart, of sharing a meal with friends. In the light of the presence that we, by different names, call God, all of life is enriched with ultimate meaning. It speaks of a time when we shall know as we are known. Now we see God as one sees riddling reflections in a mirror; but then we will see "face to face."

One of the reasons so much of our pop culture today—films, novels, raucous music—is so shallow, seeming to meld together in an amorphous, meaningless mass, is that it lacks this dimension of the eternal. In the end, nobody really cares because its inner message is that there is finally nothing there of lasting value to care about. The classics of the past, whether in art, literature, or music, were not preachy, but they were created in the light of the abiding (*sub specie aeternitatis*). They endure because they shimmer with perpetual truth.

I'm aware that you cannot prove the existence of God. But that is really of little concern. One cannot prove most important things—the love of children or spouse, the truth of a poem, a statue, a painting, or a symphony.

I know that people such as Freud have said that God is nothing more than an exalted father, and that He is just a wishfulfilment projected into the sky. But this argument goes two ways. Freud's atheism could, by his own logic, be just the projection of his own wishful thinking, the ultimate "no" to his own father.

None of this has anything to do with the surface of what we call "the news." It has everything to do with what lies beneath it.

Tension and Growth

When Prime Minister Brian Mulroney announced that Canada would not participate directly in the Star Wars research project, the decision, after months of debate, seemed to be a sign not just of national confidence, but of independence and a tough devotion to peace. Like most I greeted the headline with gratitude and applause.

Yet, looked at more closely, our apparent firmness has the consistency of a marshmallow. Indeed, the whole affair illustrates a human habit that creates havoc in our individual lives as well as in the world of foreign policy: that is, the attempt to pursue two (or more) conflicting, contradictory goals at the same time.

My interest here is with how this clash of goals and/or values causes pain, frustration, anger, depression, and sometimes serious illness in our own daily lives. But because what nations do often reflects what is going on in the minds or souls of human beings generally, our Star Wars response is a relevant place to start.

Mulroney said no to the U.S. Strategic Defense Initiative in terms of government-to-government participation. But the door was left open for full involvement in the future, and meanwhile Canadian firms that land Star Wars contracts will get all the usual tax breaks, loans, and grants. Small wonder the PM was able to say "I don't think there will be any disappointment in the White House" about our stance. Talk about trying to have your cake and eat it too!

We want to be an independent, self-respecting country; we want to promote nuclear sanity and appear peace-loving, but at the same time we desperately want to be liked by everybody, and especially by the U.S. Any of these may be commendable goals, but to try to realize them all simultaneously can only lead to a national schizophrenia. We will never solve the problem of our "Canadian identity" as long as we keep on this way.

At the personal level, one of the deepest causes of confusion for many, even most of us, at times, is rooted in the same kind of struggle. Usually, though, we fail to discern the source or sources of our discomfort, either because we have denied or repressed the conflict, or because we've been so busily immersed in the pressures of life that we've had no time to stop and ponder what exactly is going on.

For example, it is quite literally impossible to hold strong opinions on controversial subjects, and to want to be able to express them freely, and at the same time to be liked or admired by everybody. Those who cling to both of these aims have set themselves up to get hurt. You can't be a genuine parent to your children and forever have them see you as some kind of indulgent super-pal. A reasonable, truly caring father or mother knows that love involves discipline.

In fact, any human relationship of lasting value must include moments of tension or there can be no growth. This is not to say such times are to be desired or sought out. But it is a dangerous illusion of our culture that happiness is automatic; that any kind of stress or pain is necessarily an insult and injustice.

People who passionately want to be at the top of their field while seeking to be, and to be perceived as being, devoted to their family life can often find themselves in a morass of guilt and other warring emotions. Doctors, ministers, social workers, teachers—any group whose self-identity is tied up with dedicated service to others—are particularly vulnerable.

Religious faith, while often providing a unity to one's life, can also be extremely stressful when it is understood as demanding an impossible moral perfection along with a never-ending smile and a visible "inner peace." It is a recipe for trouble to affirm acceptance of one's humanity while always, in reality, denying it.

What is most helpful, I believe, is to make time at regular intervals, or whenever life seems to close in, to examine just what our goals and values, immediate and long-term, are. Setting them down on paper in order of priority can often be a turning point. Contradictions that we never realized existed can suddenly leap out at us and demand some kind of change.

It would be easy enough to quote modern psychiatrists and self-help "experts" on the importance of harmonizing one's basic objectives in life. But there is a more ancient wisdom available. This is precisely what the Sermon on the Mount means when it says: "The light of the body is the eye; if therefore thine eye be single, thy whole body shall be full of light."

Where there is no singleness of purpose, it says, the result can be darkness or confusion. It is true for countries pursuing peace; it is true for persons seeking to be truly human.

Love

Browsing in a bookstore the other day, among the myriad tomes I found one advocating a totally new world religion. Islam, Judaism, Christianity, and all the others are far too old to be of any use, the author argued in his prologue. It is time to jettison the lot.

Intrigued, I read on far enough to learn that the goal and guiding light of the proposed new faith would be one's own personal happiness. The chief moral value would be respect for others. Respect, the author said, is a much more realistic criterion for conduct than the Christian idea of love. Love is "too demanding." At a quick read, it sounded plausible enough. Certainly the role of religion in contemporary societies is open to criticism. But there are a couple of fundamental errors in supposing that some new global faith should be built on the twin pillars of the pursuit of individual happiness and respect.

Naturally we all want to be happy. But as Plato said long ago—and nearly every serious thinker since has repeated-happiness is an extremely difficult concept to define. And whatever it is, it is certain to elude us whenever we pursue it directly. Happiness is a by-product of other things, other activities, and other goals. It comes, said Plato, uncontrived, unbidden, "like the bloom on the cheek of youth." Any religion based on a direct attempt to seek happiness itself sets one off in search of a will-o'-the-wisp. As Jesus put it, by seeking always to save your life, you are certain to lose it.

Obviously this has nothing to do with putting on hair shirts or masochistically denying life's pleasures and joys. It is simple realism. Like it or not, this is how the universe and our human nature work. We are usually the happiest when we forget all about trying to be so and lose ourselves in work or play or concern for others.

When it comes to enjoining respect upon us rather than, say, the Christian concept of love, we are brought face to face with one of the commonest misunderstandings in the entire religious spectrum. The problem in a way is due to the poverty of the English language. We have only the one word, love, to express such a wide range of feelings, thoughts, and actions. Thus we can say, "I love fast cars"; "I love cross-country skiing"; "I love my parents"; "I love my husband." The word has to cover everything from the vaguest awareness of liking something, to sexual love, to the abiding affection of good friends.

When we hear the New Testament saying we are to love one another and love our neighbor as ourselves, there is too often a guilt-producing inner message that somehow we have to muster up a kind of emotional warmth and good feeling about everybody. A mass of inner clutter swarms in. This is not what is meant at all. Nowhere in the Bible does it say you are supposed to *like* everybody.

The Greek from which the modern New Testament is translated had three different words for different kinds of love: one for erotic passion (*eros*), one for the love of friends (*philia*), and one for the love of God and neighbor (*agape*). *Agape*—and, in fact, what the entire Bible means when it refers to the motive power in relationships between humans or with God—has very little to do with our feelings and everything to do with our will.

To love other people in this way means to will the very best for them and to do whatever lies in our power to make this possible. You don't have to hold them in affectionate regard or approve of their lifestyle; you don't even have to know them; you can still love them as fellow beings of equal value in God's sight.

Respect is fine as far as it goes, but essentially it preserves things very much as they are. *Agape* seeks social justice; it can change the world.

Old Age

The ancient Stoics used to say that life is like a dog tied by a leash to a moving chariot. The dog has no choice as to whether he'll move. He really only has two options: he can run relaxed and easily alongside or he can resist and be dragged, bruised and howling, to the final destination. So also with human life, they said. A person can live according to the laws of the cosmos, obeying both the God within and the God without, or he can be hauled along digging in his heels and screaming all the way.

There is a remarkable parallel between this imagery and the way we look at old age and the process of growing older in our culture. Everybody without exception is daily aging; almost everybody wants to go on living longer and longer; but nobody wants to be, or admit to being, old.

Old age, like death, is what happens to other people, not us. "My, but she's showing her age," the gossips say, avoiding the mirror all the while. It's like the doting mother who sees her son in his first parade and announces that "everybody's out of step but our John." Yet Statistics Canada projects that by the year 2000 there will be 3.3 million people in this country over the age of sixty-five, and that by 2030 this number will have nearly doubled again. If we survive, many of us will be seniors sooner than we may like to think.

Improvements are being made in income supplementation and adequate housing. But a good deal of what has now become a growth industry commercially is, when all is said and done, really a form of denial. Magazine racks and bookstores are filled with literature aimed at reassuring us that old age is more illusory than real. Here's a sampling: *The Long-Life Gourmet Cookbook, Maximum Life Span, Conquest of Death, Nutrition And Aging, Life Extension Companion, Ageproofing* (''offering a sound and easy-to-live-with diet and exercise program that let you counteract the unwanted changes in looks, health and fitness that can come with aging.") Newspapers devote entire pages to similar themes and are particularly fond of vivid accounts of the latest behavioral-psychology findings on the sex lives and "needs" of seniors.

Wonderful. But why is it that so many notables in North American society, when they finally realize they're not immortal and that the final chapter is unravelling, sound as though somehow they've been cheated, dealt an unfair, unexpected blow?

In her book *My Father, Frank Sinatra* Nancy Sinatra says her controversial parent was acutely anxious about his seventieth birthday: "His eyes fill up when he thinks about it. But, he's a young seventy . . . ."

Katharine Hepburn, Irving Layton, and Pierre Berton are only a few of the other names that come to mind when I think of those who have recently expressed negative feelings about growing older. One is reminded of the saying of Benjamin Disraeli: ''Youth is a blunder; manhood a struggle; old age a regret."

What I miss, I guess, for myself and particularly for the youth of our day, is the note of optimism, of wisdom, of meaning—the voice that tells us why it is good to be "full of days," what insights age brings that youth only dreamed of. Where are those who can say, with the Roman man of letters Cicero (106–43 B.C.), that old age is "the crown of life" and go on to tell us why? About five hundred years earlier, the Greek law-giver Solon wrote: "I grow old ever learning many things"—a thought echoed by a poet of our own era, T.S. Eliot: "Old men ought to be explorers." I also like the words of Job 12:12—"With the very old there is wisdom; and in length of days comes understanding"—and of the prophet Joel: "Your old men shall dream dreams . . . ."

Most of all, though—indeed, ever since I first knew them—I have been inspired by some words of St. Paul's. I am not one of those who is convinced that everything he wrote came straight from above, but this statement about aging rings with truthfulness and hope: "Even though our external bodies suffer the process of decay, nevertheless our true inner self is ever being made new, day by day" (II Cor. 4:16). One day, he continues, our mortality will be wholly ''swallowed up by Life."

Two realities converge here. One is that as we grow older the "things that are unseen"—the values and experiences that lie at the heart of our humanity, as opposed to looks or material possessions—can and should matter much more. The other is the sense of serenity and expectation that comes with the inner awareness, faith, and hope that old age is not a tragic ending, but the prelude to an adventure beyond words to tell.

Some will call this wishful thinking. But for me, only the expectation of a richer life to come makes proper sense of all the rest. One day I hope to be able to say: "Youth was a gift, and middle age a work of art. But old age was like a rare wine kept until the last."

Depression

According to a recent report, roughly 10 percent of Canadians will need psychiatric help in coping with the problem of depression at one time or another in their lifetime. Another 20 percent will suffer from it and be treated by their family doctor. Nobody, the study says, knows for sure how many others presenting themselves for medical attention are really dealing with depression in one of its many masks.

The physical symptoms apparently can range from back pains to high blood pressure, insomnia, or "nerves." Because of the social stigma still clinging to all forms of emotional or mental disturbance, it is much more respectable to tell a doctor about physical ailments than to admit to a depressive state.

Yet depression is one of the most ancient illnesses known, striking the rich and famous, the creative geniuses, and the most ordinary among us. Winston Churchill, with his "black dog" days, is only one example. Clergy and others engaged in counselling know that it can strike those who appear strongest on the surface as well as those who seem weaker. They know too that it can be the basic factor in the lives of many who attempt to deny it through alcohol, drugs, bed-hopping, excessive perfectionism, even obsession with work at the expense of all else.

Often depression lies behind the otherwise inexplicable acts of violence we read about daily, the cause of which is often buried rage that cannot be faced and dealt with. So long as the real source of the evil isn't faced, the effort to hide it or hold it down takes its toll on energy, health or relationships. Of course, there can be basic genetic or other real physical causes as well. Full analysis of the complex roots of depression is a matter for the professionals in the field.

My concern here is the reality that there are countless thousands in our midst who may not know where to turn or what to do; who are genuinely suffering and who need help, encouragement, and understanding. I'm not talking about those who feel a little blue on Monday mornings at the office. There are normal ups and downs for all of us in the course of living. These can result from the weather, the mood in our workplace, or the news of the day.

The "feel" of a true depression can only be known by those who have either experienced it or who have tried to work with those in its grip. There is an almost clinical account, written some twenty-five hundred years ago, in a number of the Psalms. One frequently cited is Psalm 22, with its description of feeling God-forsaken: "I am poured out like water, and all my bones are out of joint; my heart . . . is like melting wax. My strength is dried up . . . ."

The core feeling seems to be that there is no end in sight, that this is how the person has always felt and always will—as Anglicans sing, in a different context, "As it was in the beginning, is now, and ever shall be." This is often accompanied by an acute sense of loneliness, of being different, of being trapped. Some say they feel a sense of impending doom or of inability to decide even the smallest of issues.

Clearly this is a kind of living hell. When someone is suffering it, there is no help in saying, "Relax, you've got everything going for you." Often the only good advice is to seek professional counselling.

Realizing that you or a loved one are depressed and then acting to seek the help of a trusted friend, minister, psychiatrist, or other clinical counsellor will not instantly solve the dilemma of a depression. But it is the important first step towards insight and recovery.

The depression will inevitably pass. That is the good news. The even better news is that, properly faced and understood, depression has what some psychoanalysts have called "secret strength." That is, it can be a formative stage in further growth and self-understanding. For further reading on this theme, I recommend *The Secret Strength of Depression*, by Frederic F. Flach, M.D.

Anxiety

A middle-aged lady wrote recently asking how to deal with fear in her life. She describes no specific phobia, such as fear of heights, or open spaces, but rather "an ill-defined, almost constant sense of anxiety." She said her pastor and the other leaders at her church had urged her to pray about her problems—as if she had not already done so time and time again. The truth is that there are some things one ought not to pray about at all. To pray about fear or anxiety can be a sure way of focussing on them and underscoring the problem further.

It is fine to pray for courage and tenacity in the face of hardship; most clergy would agree that meditation on some of the great faith affirmations of the Bible could be of immense help; nobody denies that the sacraments or other spiritual aids are sources of inner strength to those with faith in them. However, simply to tell someone troubled by ongoing *angst* or even dread to pray harder is to add a feeling of condemnation to an already harried soul.

I am not a psychotherapist, but years of pastoral counselling taught me what all psychotherapists know: that fears and anxieties have to be faced, their causes known. Often a trusted friend or minister can be of assistance. In the case of the woman who wrote to me the problem seemed somewhat deeper, and so I recommended she seek the advice of a professional clinical counsellor or a psychiatrist.

What is extraordinary in our society is the negative attitude that still prevails with regard to psychiatry—particularly among religious people and communities. When members of the American Psychiatric Association met in Washington in 1986 they were addressed by the controversial Roman Catholic theologian Hans Küng. He told them that too many psychiatrists take a repressive attitude towards religion and questioned whether it was possible that some, though not all, of the neuroses of our times could be diagnosed as the result of "spiritual trauma" and repression of deep spiritual feelings. Certainly.

However, psychiatrists could well come back at Küng and charge that religion in general, and the churches in particular, have for their part tried to repress psychiatry by giving it a bad name. Having once had the cure of souls all to itself, the Church sometimes views the high priests of the secular approach to mental and emotional health with ill-concealed envy, or worse. In fact, all forms of healing—exercise, nutrition regimens, relaxation techniques, meditation, whatever—have a role in helping people deal with tensions, anxieties, and fears.

The basic spiritual law, of course, is the one expressed by all the world's great faiths: that one should live in the present rather than regretting the past and fearing the future. As Dr. Gerald Jampolsky, the noted psychiatrist and author of several books on the emotions of love and of fear, has said, the ultimate way to deal with fear is to limit one's thoughts to the present. It is foolish and destructive to believe that the past predicts the future. For him, to learn to live in the present, and to think of the future as an extension of that moment, is to have begun to open oneself to healing.

V

MISCELLANY

Going Home

I felt the roughness of the fieldstone wall and leaned over to see the rushing waters of the *burn*—a small creek—below. Then I remembered the sharp rap on the ear I once got from the local squire for dropping a good portion of that wall into the stream to show the other boys what Niagara Falls looked like.

That was over twenty-five years ago. The miracle to me, standing there in County Tyrone listening to the babbling water and scenting the unforgettable hint of turf smoke in the air, was that nothing seemed to have changed. It was like Rip Van Winkle in reverse: as if the village of Tullyhogue and its surroundings had been sleeping while the world outside—my world—had swept on. Now I had stepped, as if by time machine, back to my roots.

Just a few hours before, we had left Belfast, a city of tears and shattered dreams, far behind as our car wound up and around the green slopes of the Cave Hill. We were heading first north, then westwards, deep into the fragrant countryside of Northern Ireland. As the sun broke out over the Glens of Antrim to the east and lit the rain-sodden fields and hills with glory, my heart had felt a lifting surge of joy.

You can scarcely get a more vivid contrast than to spend a week studying the effects of ten years of strife on the children of Belfast, where terror stalks the streets, and then to escape to one of the most pastoral, peaceful landscapes on the face of the earth.

Everything conspired to delight the eye—the green of the tiny, hedge-ringed fields was even more vibrant than I had recalled; quaint whitewashed cottages sat perched on the mountainsides and nestled in folds of the hills. Fat cattle and sheep browsed shoulder to shoulder in the pastures and winding, sparkling rivers ran beneath old stone-arched bridges on their journey to the sea.

Past the gleaming waters of Loch Neagh, where salmon fishermen tended their nets, we drove, and on into the heart of the hills and glens of County Tyrone, birthplace of my father and his forefathers for more than four hundred years.

I should give a word of explanation. I was born in Canada of Irish immigrant parents. But Tullyhogue, a little village sixty miles from Belfast, was for a large part of my early life, especially during student days at Oxford, my second home.

My grandfather, a man with mischievous blue eyes and a walrus moustache—singed more than once from his habit of reading in bed at night with a candle on his chest—was the village blacksmith, postmaster, and bandmaster. He could get music out of any instrument he picked up and would walk or ride on a bicycle for miles around teaching bands in other villages as well.

My chest almost burst with pride when, at the age of ten, he first allowed me to wield the mighty bellows in his forge. As the flames roared, the air was filled with the clangor of the hammer, and the horseshoe in the tong glowed white with heat. Once the horse was shod there was always time for gossip with the farmers who made it a routine to gather there.

The forge, an oblong, low-roofed, whitewashed building at the crossroads around which the tiny hamlet is clustered, is still there. But it is silent. Gone are the rich smells of horses and burning metal mingled with the aroma of my grandfather's pipe. The great anvil lies disused in one corner surrounded by odds and ends left over from later days when my Uncle Bob, my mentor in the art of fly-fishing, used to run a modern garage.

But little else has changed.

True, both grandparents had long since gone to their rest in the family burying place, Donnarisk, a round, humpy cemetery with a high stone wall, on a hillside visible from Tullyhogue's main street. But there is hardly a wrought-iron gate for miles around that does not yet bear the initials TWH, which were my grandfather's and also happen to be mine.

Standing with my coat collar up in a vain attempt to ward off a soft Irish mizzle that made the holly hedges glisten as if freshly waxed, I stopped at one such gate. As I read the inscribed letters, the sounds, smells, and warmth of the old forge flooded to mind. I could see once again those brawny arms and feel my own dawning sense of manhood as I fanned the fire. A sense of nostalgia, but no regrets. Rather, a quiet sense of joy.

As a youth I was a constant rover over the surrounding hills with dogs and gun, and I knew the haunts of trout and salmon in every neighboring river and stream. Since most of my relatives still lived nearby, I spent all my vacations from university in England there.

One was supposed to study. But my Uncle Bob's two terriers would sit patiently looking in at the window as I labored, waiting for the slightest movement towards the cupboard with the guns and fishing rods. Even a glance at it was enough to send them into paroxysms of anticipation. And often the temptation to be out of doors would prove too strong to fight.

I don't believe in reincarnation, of dogs or anybody else, but the two successors of my former hunting companions, Rex and Darky, turned out to be their "spitting image," as they say here. Or, even more Irish: "They're more like them than they were like themselves!"

Together with some of the village children, including ten-year old Tommy Harpur, a son of one of my cousins, I visited the old abandoned quarry and picked ripe hazelnuts just as we used to long ago, while the two young terriers put rabbits out of the thickets in all directions.

Then we tramped across the rain-soaked fields to the Priory Well, in a corner of a pasture not far from the cemetery. As we lay on our stomachs we could peer down into the crystal waters and see the white sand at the bottom boiling as the spring bubbled up. It was moving to think that it had done that during all my years of absence—indeed throughout the centuries since the Priory monks of the Middle Ages first cleared the sod away and built the encircling drystone wall.

Tullyhogue itself, about three miles from the market town of Cookstown, lies in a saucer-like depression in the hills—a village of less than forty houses and cottages huddling together for company. The name means "Hill of the Youth" and is derived from a high, forest-topped hill immediately to the east on which the ancient kings of Ulster, the O'Neills, used to be crowned.

Like many similar dominating hills throughout the British Isles, it was fortified from prehistoric times, and today you can still see the double earthen walls that ring the crest. Like my father and his before him, I had often played at cowboys and Indians or Robin Hood among the ancient beech and oak trees inside the inner rampart. It was a strange feeling to walk the outer wall again and see the places where we had once whiled away so many hours excavating in the hope of finding ancient coins, swords, and arrowheads as visions of heroic battles fired our over-eager imaginations. The view from the top is breath-takingly beautiful. On one horizon lie the waters of Loch Neagh; on another, the gloomy moors atop Slieve Gallion, the mountain where we had often hunted partridge and snipe.

As I gazed at it the most poignant memory of my youth came storming back. I had been hunting with my uncle's favorite gun, a double-barrelled shotgun with a polished cherrywood stock. Late in the day I shot a rabbit but only succeeded in wounding it.

It screamed in fear, the most blood-curdling sound I had ever heard, and as I rushed to try and put it out of its misery I vowed I would never hunt again. I looked in vain for a stick or stone with which to kill it and, finding none, decided to use the gun butt. I unloaded the remaining cartridge and swung the weapon at the rabbit's head. It struck, but unfortunately it hit the ground as well and, while the rabbit was dead, the cherry stock had broken at the grip.

I felt devastated at the thought of trying to explain that to my uncle. But he was remarkably calm about it when the moment came, and today, duly spliced together by an expert, the gun still stands in the cupboard. I handled it with mingled feelings during my visit home. It reminded me of the two important lessons I had learned that day: the power of forgiveness and the evil of "sport" hunting. In all the intervening years I have never fired another shot.

Closer, near the foot of the fort hill, I could see the Tullywig-gan River as it tumbled down through narrow glens to join the Balinderry River—some of the best salmon water in the world. A host of magic, almost fairy-tale names came suddenly to mind as I caught a glimpse of the turretted towers of Killymoon Castle a couple of miles away and of the woods at the Loughrey estate where Dean Jonathan Swift once lived and where his cottage still stands, overlooking a marvelous waterfall.

To the north I could see Desertcreat Church, the Church of

Ireland (Anglican) chapel where all our family records are. Set among somber yew trees on a knoll just above the river, the spot has had a Christian place of worship on it since A.D. 485, the time of St. Patrick's mission among these very hills. The choirmaster used to grow red in the face and mutter fierce threats when we choirboys used to reverse the refrain to one of the Lenten hymns: "to be a grim pill" instead of "to be a pilgrim."

Down the hedgerowed lane to the south was the little school where I once taught for a week when the teacher was taken ill. The children had sat round-eyed as I told them of the Canadian north and the three summers I had spent with the Cree at Big Trout Lake, one of our most remote Ontario reserves; they simply couldn't get enough about huskies, and trapping, and travelling by canoe. I remembered also being as happy as they were when an official holiday was declared for the potato harvest and we were able to leave the classroom and help gather in the crop. Muddy hands, cheeks red with wind and mist, and appetites enormous at tea-time!

The school hasn't changed an iota since, except for a fresh batch of apple-cheeked youngsters. Some of the former pupils now have families of their own and live nearby, but most have been scattered to the corners of the globe.

Best of all, though, was an afternoon spent fishing the Tullywiggan once again. My cousin David Adams knew the people at the castle, and so we got permission to fish an incredible reach of water filled with a series of rapids and deep, dark pools.

We both laughed as we remembered a time when we would never have stopped to ask permission. Poaching was more in our line as boys. Once, in the dead of night, when another lad and I had gone down to the river with a lantern to see if the salmon were up, this same cousin had scared the life out of us by pretending to be the game warden. He gave a shout as we crouched by the river's edge. Overcome by panic, we doused the light and took to our heels through thorn hedges and streams, over fences, reckless of damage to either clothes or skin. We were indeed a sorry sight by the time we reached home and bed.

This time Adams used a fly rod and I relied on spinning tackle. We missed several fine salmon but soon had a dozen of the finest speckled trout I have ever seen. If anything, the fishing had got better since I last had wet a line there. Oblivious of the drizzling rain and gusting wind, we fished until dark. I was sorry to have to leave, especially since my cousin kept assuring me that "the best fishing's just beginning now." But I had promises to keep.

Later that same evening, a star-filled night wrapped in the deep silence of all rural retreats, I was taken to Tullyhogue's social center, McQueen's Halfway House, just across from the forge.

The pub's two small rooms, one of them reserved for darts, were crowded with welcoming faces, presided over by McQueen himself and his beaming wife. Neither seemed to have aged a wrinkle. I was surrounded by cousins, distant relatives, and former friends. They were full of remarks—"Look at the size of him; what a pity he's not in the police!"—and regrets: "You'll not be here for the pheasant shoot then? The woods are full of them this year." It was impossible to buy either oneself or anyone else a drink, yet one's glass was somehow never empty.

When people think or talk of Northern Ireland today they think, alas, of violence. Its grim face is there and I had looked it in the eye in Belfast. But there is another side to the story. For me the memory can never fade of dreaming rivers, cozy hearths, and happy faces among the green hills of Tyrone.

Risk with a Purpose

There have been several sad stories lately about teenagers being maimed or killed while riding atop elevators in highrise buildings. Such accidents are every parent's worst nightmare, and my first response was alarm and outrage at the stupidity of such behavior.

But then, quite suddenly, my mind did a back-flip, and memory took me back to a golden month of May many years ago, at Oxford, when I did something that was not very bright myself. I had been out rowing in an "eight" all afternoon, had just finished tea, and was getting down to an essay that was due next day for my tutor when a fellow student burst into my room. His name was Dawson and he had a wild light in his eye. "They say you brought a canoe with you from Canada," he said. I told him I had—a light, collapsible craft made by the same company that made the Link Trainers for pilots during World War II. When you removed the canvas sheath, you simply unlinked the various sections and then stowed them in your car trunk or in the baggage compartment of the train.

Reassured about the existence of the canoe, Dawson promised he would only take a few moments of my time and proceeded to unroll a large-scale map of medieval Oxford.

"There it is," he said excitedly, pointing to a blue line running from the Isis (as the Thames is called in its upper reaches), north of the city, straight under the city center to connect once more with the river at the southern edge of town. He said the line showed what had once been a major sewer for the university centuries ago. With a pencil he traced the way the river made a right angle as it bent around the ancient town; the tunnel, or sewer, made the hypotenuse or third side. Dawson then revealed his scheme.

The tunnel apparently was no longer a sewer—it had not been since the modern era. It was now simply an overflow from the river; in fact, it made a picturesque stream where it exited into the rose garden of Christ Church College, before running by the university meadows and back into the Isis. Just that afternoon, in the library, Dawson had discovered that, during his stint at Oxford, Lawrence of Arabia had swum up its length, under the colleges and town center to the entrance. We, he said, should do it by canoe.

I ought to have thrown him out. Instead, two days later we portaged the canoe from the River Cherwell, where I kept it, along the Broad Walk, with its arching elms, to the rose garden. As a stunned gardener gaped, we lowered the canoe, climbed down into it, and disappeared into a round black opening about six feet high. The water was shallow, the current slight—not enough to matter.

Before long our flashlight quit; the tunnel shrank in diameter. But it was impossible to turn back. At times there would be a manhole to the surface and a sound of traffic. The rest was darkness and slime and fear. As the song says, "Everybody's got to be somewhere." I'd have given a lot to have been anywhere else but there. And we were there a long time.

The worst part was that I had now started to do some of the

thinking work I should have done before agreeing to such craziness. The horrible thought occurred: what if they suddenly open the locks up river? What if there's a flash flood? We'd drown like rats or else be shot backwards out into the garden like the cork out of a champagne bottle. Eventually we rounded a bend and saw the almost-despaired-of light. By the time we emerged, soaked, grimy, and exhausted, I had seen a light of a different kind.

We had perhaps risked our lives. We had certainly risked being sent down in disgrace from the university, since entering the sewer was specifically banned. But none of it had been to any real purpose. We had been fools and we both knew it.

I realized a truth that has stuck with me ever since, and it's one I wish we could communicate to every teenager: life is essentially a matter of taking risks; but, as missionary-doctor Bob McClure says (and who knows better?), they should be risks "with a purpose."

What's more, let it not be just any purpose—selfishness, vanity, greed, or showing off. Genuine risk-taking, the kind that enlarges our horizons and deepens our maturity, demands a purpose worthy of our best or highest selves. It's not enough to scold young people with a list of don'ts—they need to be challenged to take risks that count. For themselves and for others.

Weddings

In all the books and articles devoted to weddings, little if anything is ever said from the point of view of a perpetually key participant: the officiating priest, rabbi, or minister. Everybody blithely supposes he or she is simply performing a pleasant duty in return for an honorarium and a free meal. Nobody is aware of the risks and hazards involved. Having performed several hundred weddings myself, I vividly remember them all.

Unfortunately for me, the press became involved in my very first wedding. I had just been made a deacon, it took place in a quaint rural church, my summer charge, and the bride was my sister. I still have the small clipping from the Toronto *Telegram* with its glaring headline: "Brother marries sister!" It was most unAnglican, but my bishop kept his thoughts to himself.

Later, my first wedding at the fashionable church where· I began as curate, after being made a priest, was not without its problems either. The families on both sides were extremely wealthy and prominent in the parish; the preparations and trimmings were lavish. I was understandably nervous as I waited with the groom and best man in the study for the buzzer signalling the bride's arrival.

The church was packed with the would-be cream of society, complete with top hats, swallow-tailed coats, and enough mink to make a jacket for a battleship. Eager to impress, I gave it my best shot and felt a surge of self-congratulation as the pair finally went down the aisle and the bells pealed.

I was pulling my surplice off, intending to take a short stroll before driving to the nuptial feast, when the organist made a cryptic comment.

"Do you suppose they're really married?" he enquired with feigned innocence.

Stunned, I said weakly, "What's the joke?"

He brought over his prayer-book and, pointing to the central part of the marriage service, where the minister joins the couple's hands and pronounces them to be man and wife ("Those whom God hath joined . . . let no man put asunder"), he said: "You left that out. In fact, you skipped the whole page."

I sank in a chair as waves of mortification swept over me. I could imagine what was being said in the limousines as shocked parents, relatives, and friends reeled at the omission. I went to the reception expecting abuse or at least cold stares. To my amazement, I was received with charm and congratulated on a "splendid show." It was hard to realize I had just blown the parish wedding of the year.

When it finally dawned on me that nobody other than the organist had been following the words at all, nobody had noticed the great lacuna, it gave me food for thought for a long time to come. So much for the illusion they had all been there because of what Anglicans like to think of as their "incomparable liturgy."

Once, when I finally got my own parish in Scarborough, the bride's mother had taken her place, the groom stood before me, and the bride was about to make her entrance, when a very drunk, very untidy man lurched noisily into a center seat.

He began to talk to those nearby in a loud voice and with the instant familiarity only alcohol can induce. I was prepared to overlook all this until I saw he had been followed by a huge, equally shabby mongrel, which he was coaxing to sit beside him on the pew. I put the ceremony on hold, walked down, and whispered: "Please get that dog out of here."

He said, "If it isn't good enough for my dog, it isn't good enough for me." That did it. Trying to look pastoral but taking a grip on him I hoped my robes might cover, I lifted him out of the seat and through the doorway.

I got back to the chancel and nodded to the organist to begin. By the time the bride started her march, the evicted man's shouts that he was going to get his gang and return for revenge were drowned out by the joyous music.

Some guests said later they thought it all very original. I thought of asking my bishop for danger pay.

Signs of Hope

If you're one of the lucky people who have had a lifelong love affair with nature and the outdoors, it's easy to get discouraged these days. I find it hard to pick up a newspaper without being told another chapter in the scandalous story of how we are fouling our planetary nest. At times the tragic accounting of acid rain, radioactive waste, the destruction of wildlife habitats and of entire species, seems more than one can bear.

As with the horrors of world hunger and poverty, the only way to keep sane and balanced about it all is to do whatever one can to help while at the same time keeping a sharp eye peeled for every sign of hope, no matter how small.

For example, just as I was getting up this morning I heard a sound that has gladdened and haunted the mind of humanity since the very dawn of creation. There may be more sting left in this winter yet, but the cry of a lone Canada goose winging low over our home has once again served notice that spring in all its release and glory is about to burst forth again. As I write, the gander has been joined by a flock of about twenty others, and they are taking off and landing with wild cries on a patch of melt out in the center of the lake.

It is encouraging to realize that there are in fact more Canada geese in southern Ontario now than there were when the first settlers arrived from Europe.

Another sign of hope came quite unexpectedly earlier this week. I was walking in from the highway, taking the shorter, winter route—a snowmobile trail beside a frozen creek and then across the ice of the lake to the north shore where I live.

To my dismay, I saw a large backhoe and several men in parkas at one of the last remaining wild spots, a swampy field where ducks and geese nest, near where the lake empties out to become the East Humber River.

Imagine my relief when I discovered that they were a team from the Ministry of Natural Resources and their aim was not to desecrate one more natural habitat but to atone for past mistakes by one of the most imaginative projects I have heard of for some time. They were creating a criss-crossing series of wide, shallow ditches to provide spawning grounds for northern pike. The tiny islands being formed in the process would make even safer nesting sites for waterfowl than before. As an ardent fisherman who has of late lost much of his old enthusiasm for the sport because of all the pollution and contamination, I invited the young fisheries biologist to stop by at our place later that day to explain the scheme.

It was fascinating. I knew our lake, part of a chain of kettle lakes formed by glacial melting ten thousand years ago—and only twenty-five miles from the heart of Toronto—had pike and bass in it. But it was a stunning surprise to learn he had trapped (and released) a pike that was 57 inches long and about 32 pounds in weight. Another, he said, was 41 inches. And, he continued, there were lots of largemouth bass in the 4- to 5-pound range.

The pike, however, are in real danger; since a flood control dam was placed in the outflow creek, in 1979, they have not been able to spawn. It seems pike only spawn on freshly flooded vegetation during spring run-off. The newly created dikes and ditches are to form an artificial wetland where this can happen once again. What is most exciting is that, since the whole watershed of which our lake is part is a microcosm of the Great Lakes system, what the biologists are researching and discovering here has importance for restoration of lost wetlands and fisheries over a vast region.

Significantly, the pike project, along with similar experiments at a nearby wilderness-type lake kept solely for research, is funded by all levels of government. Local fishing clubs, the lake dwellers, and all the children in neighboring schools are to be involved in various ways. For example, the children will not only learn about the importance of habitat to fish and waterfowl, but be enlisted to help prevent vandalism or injury to the pike during the actual spawning.

The fact that a natural cycle that began ten thousand years ago is going to go on into the future fills me with hope. Think of it. Before God called Abraham to leave his home in Ur in Mesopotamia, before any of the Bible was even written, the pike were living in this lake. It gives you a sense of perspective, especially if you are one of those who believe the secret of living lies, as Edith Wharton once wrote, in being "interested in big things, and happy in small ways."

Gordon Sinclair

A young priest just out of seminary was in a panic as he prepared for his first Sunday in his parish. He phoned his bishop and asked, "What shall I preach about?" His wise mentor replied, "Preach about God and preach about fifteen minutes."

This column is about God—and about Gordon Sinclair whose outspoken, familiar voice, was stilled forever on May 17, 1984. Sinclair—"Sinc," as many knew him—is missed by all who loved his flamboyant style, his gutsy probings, his sense of what makes news, and his keen nose for hypocrisy whether in the name of God or of Mammon.

Organized religion ought to feel the loss of Sinclair more than most because he was a kind of "noble enemy" who acted as a gadfly to keep it on the track. Unlike many who preen themselves and talk about their agnosticism Sinclair held the "God question" to be of central importance. He read his Bible constantly—more than many of the believers he loved to challenge—and there was a sincerity about his questioning that was sometimes hidden by the bluntness of his approach.

I had the privilege of discussing religion with Sinclair on air a number of times and was always impressed with his genuine desire to cut through all the nonsense and get at the core of the matter. People used to warn me before such shows that Sinclair hated religion and would chew me into little pieces for all to see. I found him quite the opposite. Brash, rough-and-tumble, yes; but to me, at least, he was always courteous and gentle beneath the bluster.

I remember asking Sinc to come and talk about his agnosticism on a half-hour TV program I used to host. He vindicated my intuition that he would make the series come alive. He sat quietly while I introduced him and then proceeded to take over the interview and grill me instead of the other way around. It soon became clear that what really bothered him was the inconsistency and just plain gobbledygook of much so-called religious language ("God-talk") and conduct. He had, rightly, nothing but scorn for the kinds of quotes you often read in newspapers— "God helped me win the lottery"; "God was in his corner, boxer says"; "Plane crash kills 40—survivors say prayer saved them."

Yet I asked him: "Gordon, when you are at your Muskoka cottage in the summer and look up at the stars at night—drifting perhaps in your boat, as I've heard you tell it—do you feel this all came from a chance collision of atoms in a sort of cosmic crap-shoot eons ago?"

He replied: "No, I don't. At that point I find I must believe in a mind or a creator behind it all. I just can't go for the kind of folksy, patsy God so many seem to believe in."

In a fundamental sense, then (even though no church would have wanted to claim him, and vice versa) he was a believer. In fact, he was the kind of believer who in other times would probably have been called a prophet—one who often flays the anointed for failing to be what they claim and were meant to be.

As any student of religion knows, there are two major strands in Judeo-Christian faith, the prophetic and the cultic. Historically, these two have always been in a state of tension, even open hostility. The cultic side has to do with maintaining religious institutions, religious rites, language, taboos, and with protecting religion's vested interests and privileges.

The prophets, on the other hand, come striding out of the wilderness with a vision of God that demands constant renewal—at times very radical—of the accepted cults. Their message is geared to the reality that, if all power corrupts, religious power too can become demonic, contrary to the Word of the Lord. The Hebrew prophets, in whose tradition Jesus also came, were always the source of fresh enlightenment. While at times their message seemed negative in that they attacked error and abuse, it was essential to true spiritual health and development. Often God chose the unorthodox for this job.

The hostility Sinclair met with from the allegedly committed is the measure of how true and necessary most of his anti-cultic criticisms were. His skill as a communicator for the common man or woman gave his critique its characteristically salty sting.

Frankly, I have missed him more recently than at any time since his death. I would have liked to have heard him with the Pope on "Front Page Challenge": "Your Holiness, we hear that the Vatican is running several million dollars in the red. When are you going to show us the black side of the ledger, the billions invested by the Vatican Bank? How much are you really worth?"

Or, on the same program, asking the Anglican bishops of Canada why they can pontificate about Nicaragua while unable, after seven years, to come up with guidelines on sexuality for their members here. Or, same place, another time, demanding to know of the United Church Moderator why his and other churches sided with the strikers in the Eaton's dispute when everyone knows the churches are among the most unfair employers in the entire country.

These are not nice questions, but that was Sinclair's appeal and charm. He simply didn't care about "nice"; he cared about "real" and about "true." If his instinct up on his Muskoka Lake was true and there is a Creator God, I'm sure Gordon is now asking questions such as to make the angels smile—or blush.

Billy Graham

Billy Graham, in a recent interview with the *Washington Post*, said he is tired and feels "too many times I'm preaching from an empty well." Nevertheless, he seemed to have much of his old fire and charisma in the televised coverage of his greater Washington crusade.

Watching him perform I felt the same respect for his overall integrity and singlemindedness I always have through the years. At the same time, there was regret that his insistence on stating the same old message in the same old way seems to have robbed him of fresh insights. You could sense why he feels the well grows empty. The world has changed.

I had to smile, though. When most people think of Graham they see him as he was on TV—a tall, craggily handsome man with a huge Bible in one hand. His face is earnest, his eyes like eagles' as he pleads with vast crowds to "make a decision for Christ." But that's not the first image that leaps to my mind. Not since an incident on the eve of his June, 1978, crusade in Toronto.

I had known him for a number of years and, wanting to edge the competition, the *Star* had sent me to Minneapolis to travel up with him. We had a long interview in a hotel at the Chicago airport and then sat together on the flight to Toronto.

His patience and accessibility were impressive. People on the plane kept asking for his autograph or coming up to shake his hand, including an elderly nun in very traditional garb. He obliged them all. The following day, on the boardwalk at the Beaches, he even autographed a cigarette package for a woman in shorts and halter who had nothing else for him to write on.

I had taken him down to the lake because I knew he still jogged and wanted to get a picture of him with a Toronto back-drop similar to the famous shot of him jogging in Hyde Park, London, on the eve of his first crusade there back in the 1950s. When the photographer had the shots we wanted, we bought a couple of hot dogs each at one of the concessions and got ready to leave.

The press officer and I had moved towards the car when I noticed the photographer take Billy aside and whisper conspir-atorially in his ear. The two of them then moved off towards the water's edge, where the evangelist took off his shoes and socks. My first thought was: Good, he's going to get some shots of Graham wading, with the CN Tower as a backdrop in the distance. Then the horrible truth broke in.

There were several concrete piers or breakwaters running out at right angles to the shore, the surface of the stone in places coming flush with the surface of the lake. In fact, some gulls roosting out there seemed to be standing on the water itself. As Billy and the photographer, David Cooper, headed out on the slimy structure, both the press officer and I suddenly real-ized what was going on. The picture was going to be one of Billy Graham apparently walking on water. We tore off our shoes and socks and plunged in while shouting at them to come ashore.

Anglicans are easily embarrassed anyway, and I was profoundly embarrassed at the thought of our trying to pose one of the world's leading preachers in such a potentially scandalous way—not to mention the risk of his slipping and crippling himself to such a degree as to abort the entire crusade. His aide was furious that, as he put it, things had gotten out of hand so fast.

Graham, however, while hoping we wouldn't do anything "unwise" with the photos, seemed happy to let Cooper have his way. In the end, several pictures were taken. But when they were printed, it turned out there had been just enough of a ripple on the water to destroy the intended illusion. It was close, but the blow-ups clearly reveal he's standing on some hidden object. His followers would probably put that down to a gracious Providence. The other photographers told Cooper it was just plain bad luck. The pictures are still in the files.

Billy Graham has often been cited as one of the most admired men in North America: certainly he is the most celebrated of all contemporary preachers and evangelists. But I will always remember him as he stood there with his pants rolled up, a stub of a hot dog still in hand, humbly trying to accommodate a super-keen photographer.

The *Washington Post* reporter said there is an air of sadness, even melancholy, about Graham in repose now. If so, I'm sorry. He's perhaps the classiest religious figure I have ever met.

Christmas Amid the Ruins of Roman Splendor

Christmas, for me, has always been a season of quite extraordinary contrasts. Since I became a journalist, I have had the rare privilege of spending the eve of our celebration of the birth of Jesus in some of the world's most intriguing, beautiful, and remote places.

This year we have come to the hauntingly beautiful island of Capri. Known for centuries as the Pearl of the Sea, Capri is tiny—covering barely six square miles—but with its saw-tooth peaks, its sheer, 1000- to 1500-foot cliff faces, and its lush, tropical-type gardens and forests, all rising out of the deepest of deep-blue waters, its impact on the senses is enormous.

Situated as it is at the southern front of the Bay of Naples, just off the grandeur of the Sorrento peninsula and with a magnificent view of the Bay of Salerno and the Amalfi Coastland, it is small wonder it has been inhabited continuously from prehistoric times.

With its warm, clear waters, water caves or grottos, natural arches, and the famous Faraglioni, the three or four soaring islands just offshore where tradition says the sirens sang of yore, it has drawn the rich, the famous, and, above all, the powerful for at least 2000 years.

Most people know that Gracie Fields came here for years—her villa can still be seen below the cliffs near the choicest, most sheltered yet spectacular cul-de-sac on the entire rocky shore, the Marina Piccola.

Many, however, are unaware that 2000 years ago this jewel of natural beauty was the focus of forces and powers inextricably linked with that first Christmas in Bethlehem, and with the earliest days of Jesus and the faith that followed in his name.

High above the little piazzetta, the domed churches and white or pastel-colored houses of the town of Capri, higher even than the exquisite village of Anacapri, which spills down the upper slope of Mount Solario, there are Roman ruins that mark the villas of the mighty Caesars cited in Luke's Gospel.

Their names, which once made the ends of the earth tremble, are now part of the lessons read at every church this Christmas: the emperor Augustus who reigned from 31 B.C. to A.D. 14—he had been adopted by Julius Caesar—and his successor, Tiberius, who died in A.D. 37.

Augustus, who was revered as a god, decreed the census that St. Luke says brought Mary and Joseph from Nazareth to Bethlehem that first Christmas Eve. Intoxicated by its charm on his first visit, in 29 B.C., he added Capri to the domain of Naples, building villas on the crags with the best vistas, and he may well have been dining sumptuously here when Jesus was born in a cave-stable.

We know almost precisely the style of life he led then from touring the ruins of Pompeii and Herculaneum, across the azure waters from Capri, at the foot of Mount Vesuvius. Vesuvius' twin peak, Mount Somma, erupted violently in A.D. 79, burying

Pompeii in white-hot ashes and pumice stones and covering Herculaneum with boiling lava. Both have been excavated almost intact—with even petrified people and pets in the last throes of death. The frescoes and statues detail the magnificence, the luxury, and the pomp; they tell also of the brutality, lechery, and greed that preceded the end.

Standing on the vine-covered marble terrace at Capri's prize showpiece, the Villa St. Michele, which perches over a precipice, we were surrounded by art works from the original villa of the Caesars on this very site. Closing your eyes, you could leap back across the centuries. You could see why Augustus, bringer of peace, founder of an empire such as had never been seen before, would have cared nothing for what might be happening in Judea, his far-off fiefdom.

Tiberius, his successor, cared even less. Yet St. Luke (3:1) says it was "in the fifteenth year" of Tiberius' reign that John the Baptist began his work. Jesus taught, was crucified, and was "raised up" from the dead during the first three years of the total of ten or eleven that Tiberius was to spend as a total recluse on Capri until his death in A.D. 37.

Tiberius, who became morose and increasingly savage as he ran the whole of the then-known world from this eyrie, built twelve villas here. But his favorite was the one dedicated to Jove (Jupiter) on top of a towering spur of rock, Mount Tiberio. The king of the gods and his earthly counterpart reigned and threatened together.

Here, amidst the grandiose ruins of past splendor, as the last gold paring of sun has now slipped below the horizon and lights begin to twinkle in the velvety haze of nightfall, we can hear the soft wash of the sea and somewhere a church bell tolling. Distant Vesuvius has disappeared in the purple gloom. The Villa Jovis suddenly feels filled with ancient ghosts and forgotten echoings reverberate around worn columns.

Augustus and Tiberius, not to mention their successors who were to live lavishly in these same villas—poor mad Caligula, Nero who, tradition says, made martyrs of both St. Peter and St. Paul—would have laughed aloud had anyone suggested to them that their empire would decay and vanish. They would have derided the thought than an obscure Jew and the movement in his name would change history and human hearts as Christianity, whatever its distortions or mistakes, has done.

Like many of us today, they would have scorned the view that things of the spirit ultimately will always vanquish those who trust in naked force or anything else. But that really is the message of Christmas: the divine Spirit is love, the most powerful energy in the universe.

Later, as we are about to leave the island, I have to smile. As if on cue, I overhear our guide, Mario, telling a member of the tour how he and his family celebrate Christmas Eve: "The youngest child in the family puts baby Jesus in the crêche . . . ." The old story is new again.

References

Batchelor, Edward, Jr., ed. *Abortion: The Moral Issues*. New York: Pilgrim, 1982.

Catholic Theological Society of America. *Human Sexuality: New Directions in American Catholic Thought*. New York: Doubleday, 1979 .

Ellis, Albert. *How to Live With and Without Anger*. Secausus, NJ.: Lyle Stuart, 1985.

Flach, Frederic F. *The Secret Strength of Depression*. New York: Bantam, 1986.

Fox, Matthew. *Western Spirituality: Historical Roots, Ecumenical Routes*. Santa Fe: Bear and Co. 1981.

————*Whee! We, Wee All the Way Home: A Guide to a Sensual Prophetic Spirituality*. Santa Fe: Bear and Co. 1981.

Lonergan, Anne, and Richards, Caroline, eds. *Thomas Berry and the New Cosmology*. Mystic, Conn.: Twenty-third Publications, 1987.

Maxwell, Fr. John. *Slavery and the Catholic Church*. Chichester: B. Rose, 1975.

Morgentaler, Henry. *Abortion and Contraception*. Toronto: General Publishing, 1981.

Nichols, Peter. *The Pope's Divisions*. Miami: Brown, n.d.

Peck, M. Scott. *The Road Less Travelled*. New York: Simon and Schuster, 1978.

Ruether, Rosemary. *Faith and Fraticide: The Theological Roots of Anti-Semitism*. New York: Harper and Row, 1974.

Russell, Bertrand. *Why I Am Not a Christian*. New York: Touchstone Books, 1967.

Russell, Peter. *The Global Brain: Speculations on the Evolutionary Leap to Planetary Consciousness*. Los Angeles: J.P. Tarcher, 1983.

Short, Robert. *Something to Believe In*. New York: Harper and Row, 1977.

Swimme, Brian. *The Universe is a Green Dragon: A Cosmic Creation Story*. Santa Fe: Bear and Co. 1984.

Taheri, Amir. *The Spirit of Allah: Khomeini and the Islamic Revolution*. Bethesda, MD: Adler and Adler, 1986.

Tavris, Carol. *Anger: The Misunderstood Emotion*. New York: Simon and Schuster, 1984.

Van der Post, Laurens. *Dark Eye in Africa*. London: Hogarth, 1955.

Weatherhead, Leslie. *The Christian Agnostic*. Nashville: Abingdon Press, 1979.

Whitehead, Alfred North. *Dialogues of Alfred North Whitehead*. Westport, Conn.: Greenwood, 1977.

Index